TIME

in the
Life of a Muslim

YUSUF AL-QARADAWI

Translated by
Abu Maimounah Ahmad bin Muhammad Bello

Ta-Ha Publishers Ltd.
1 Wynne Road
London SW9 0BB
United Kingdom

Copyright © Taha Publishers Ltd. 1421AH / 2000CE

Published in September 2000 by:

Taha Publishers Ltd.
1 Wynne Road
London SW9 0BB
United Kingdom

Website: http://www.taha.co.uk
Email: sales@taha.co.uk

By: Yusuf al-Qaradawi
Translated by: Ahmad Bello
Edited by: A. Johnston

A catalogue record of this book is available from the British Library.

ISBN 1 84200 007 1

Printed and bound by: De-Luxe Printers
Website: http://www.de-luxe.com
Email: printers@de-luxe.com

CONTENTS

Translator's Forward

This book is an English translation, from the original Arabic, of Dr. Yusuf al-Qaradawi's *"Al-Waqtu fiy Hayatil Muslim"*.

Whoever is not grateful to men is not grateful to Allah:

I am grateful to Col. Abdulmalik Jibril and Lt. Bala Ahmad Musa who assisted in getting the Arabic version of this book; to Mal. Iliyasu Maitala who arranged the typing, and Mrs. Evelyn Ekata Ikhiwu (nee Orumen) who typed the manuscript. Mal. Kabir M. Yari, Rabilu Murtala Muhammad, Sa'idu Abubakar Wushishi and Sani Yahaya Abba have taken a keen interest in helping to improve the quality of this work. Mal. Abdulkareem A. Adesokan and Adebola Mustapha Animasaun, have rendered their assistance in trying to get in touch with Dr. Qaradawi to obtain his formal permission to publish this translation of his original work. Dr. Muhtar Bello, my brother, and Mal. Dahiru Muhammad have cheerfully made their resources available to me in stocking my library and providing useful reference materials for this work. Sister Ayshah Johnston of Taha Publishers has been singularly instrumental in getting this work published. My wife, Hawwaa Abdurrahman Mora, has rendered her support throughout the preparation of this book. She has listened to and read different translations of many passages to help me choose the best. Dr. Qaradawi has kindly given his consent for the translation. To all these and others not mentioned, I wish to acknowledge my debt of gratitude. I pray Allah to bless and reward them all.

It is the desire of Dr. Qaradawi that translated works should not be literal. Rather, they should be faithfully accurate, eloquent and skillfully engaging. I have tried to make this translation so. If I have succeeded, it is with the help of Allah; if I have failed, I take full responsibility and pray to Allah to forgive me and protect His servants from my error. I am exceedingly grateful to Allah, however, if one soul may be guided aright by one good paragraph in this my humble effort. All praise is due to Allah through Whose grace all good things are accomplished.

Ahmad Bello – Lagos, Nigeria.

In The Name Of Allah, Al-Rahman, Al-Rahim [1]

Preface

All praise and gratitude are due to Allah, by Whose grace all good (deeds) are accomplished. Peace and blessings be upon His Messenger (Muhammad) who has been sent as a special mercy to all creatures, and upon members of his household, his companions and all those who may be guided by his Sunnah to the Day of Judgement.

These are but a few pages that I have written on the (divine) gift of "Time", its value in the life of a Muslim and a Muslim's obligations towards it. I have been prompted to this by my knowledge and awareness of the profound interest taken in "Time" by Islam in its Book (the Qur'an) and its Tradition (the Sunnah of the Prophet).

I have been equally prompted to write by what I have observed in the attitude of our Muslim forebears in the early centuries of Islam— and those were the golden centuries— an attitude which displays a rigorous frugality over their Time which surpasses the tight-fistedness of their successors over money and property; a passionate parsimony over Time, whose harvest was useful knowledge, excellent deeds, blessed Jihad, manifest conquests and a civilisation which is lofty and deeply-rooted.

I have yet again been prompted to write due to a phenomenon I have been living and experiencing in the Muslim world today. It is the abuse and misuse of Time and the dissipation of human life and energy, which

---

[1] These two attributes of Allah, *Ar-Rahman* and *Ar-Rahim*, are difficult, if not impossible, to render into single English equivalents. Both derive from the quality of mercy and compassion. *"Ar-Rahman"* denotes Allah's attribute of mercy which, by virtue of His being the Creator, Lord and Sustainer, encompasses everything and everyone: the evil and the pious alike. On the other hand, however, *"Ar-Rahim"* denotes Allah's attribute of compassion, which, in the Life Hereafter, is limited to His pious servants only. — Translator.

has grown from the level of simple idiocy and matured into outright lunacy until, with time, Muslims have been eased into the passenger seat of the chariot of life whence they were once in the driver's seat. This has been made possible because they have neither sufficiently worked for the flourishing of their earthly life, as secular men do, nor for the flourishing of their life hereafter, as devout people do. Nay, they have destroyed the Two Worlds and have been denied the "Two Good Things"! If they had knowledge and comprehension they would certainly have worked just as assiduously for the benefit of this world as if they would live forever, and worked just as assiduously for the benefit of the life hereafter as if they would die on the morrow. They would have made that comprehensive supplication of the Qur'an their motto:

"Our Lord! Give us good in this World and good in the Hereafter. And save us from the torment of the Fire." —(Suratul Baqarah 2: 201)

May it come to pass that Time will teach the Muslims, and the alternation of Day and Night will awaken them— if they possess the quintessence of sense:

"Behold! In the creation of the heavens and the earth, and the alternation of Night and Day, there are indeed signs for men of understanding: Men who remember Allah standing, sitting, and lying down on their sides, and contemplate the (wonders of) creation in the heavens and the earth, (and say): 'Our Lord! Not in vain have Thou created (all) this! Glory be to Thee! Therefore give us salvation from the torment of the Fire. Our Lord! Any whom Thou do admit to the Fire, truly Thou cover with shame, and never will the wrongdoers find any helpers! Our Lord! We have indeed heard the call of one calling (us) to Faith, 'Believe ye in your Lord!', and so we believed. Our Lord! Forgive us our sins, blot out from us our iniquities, and take to Thyself our souls in the company of the righteous. Our Lord! Grant us what Thou did promise unto us through Thy messengers, and save us from shame on the Day of Judgment: for Thou never break Thy promise."

(Suratu Aal 'Imran 3: 190-193)

Characteristics Of Time

Time has certain peculiarities and characteristics, which it is necessary for us to properly understand, so that we may behave in accordance with them.

1) Its Transience

Time is so transient that it vanishes away like the cloud and passes away like the wind, regardless of whether it is the Time of ease and happiness (which appears to pass quickly), or the Time of difficulty and grief (which appears to be slow-footed). A poet says:

> *"Years pass by with beloved ones in happiness,*
> *As if days they were in their briefness,*
> *Came days later of separation from beloved ones,*
> *As if years for their length indeed they were,*
> *Those tenants (of Time) pass away as did those years,*
> *As if the years and the peoples but dream they were".*

However long a man may live on this earth, his life is indeed short as long as death is the ultimate end of every living creature. May Allah have mercy on the poet who says: *"If death be the end of life then it makes no difference whether life is long or short!"* At the time of death the years, as well as their episodes, which man has lived through and experienced will assuredly shrivel so much so that they will appear as if they were but a few, dazzling moments.

A story is told about the Elder of the Messengers of Allah, Nuh (Noah), peace be upon him. It is that the angel of death came to him to take his life after he had lived for over one thousand years[2], before and after the Great Deluge. He inquired from him, *"O the longest living prophet! How did you find the world?* He replied, *"Like a house having two*

---

[2] The Noble Qur'an says: *"We did send Nuh to his people, and he tarried among them a thousand years less fifty"*. (Suratul Ankabut 29: 14). —Translator.

doors; I entered through one of them and made my exit through the other!!".

Whether or not this story is true, it nevertheless illustrates an established reality, which is the shrivelling and diminishing of lifetimes at the moment of death. In fact, it will come to pass at the time of Resurrection that man will be shown the shortness and insignificance of what has gone by, as Allah Ta'ala says:

"The Day they see it, (it will be) as if they had tarried but a single evening, or (at most till) the following morn!"
(Suratun Nazi'at 79: 46)

And in another ayah, *"And on the Day when He will gather them together: (it will be) as if they had tarried but an hour of a day: they will recognise one another."* (Suratu Yunus 10: 45)

2) Whatever Vanishes of Time will neither Return nor be Replaced

This is another oddity of Time. Each day that passes, and each hour and each moment that vanishes away is impossible to retrieve, and therefore impossible to be replaced. This is the phenomenon that al-Hasan al-Basri most eloquently describes in his statement: *"There is not a single day which is ushered in by its morning twilight except it calls out, 'O son of Adam! I am a new creature, and I am a witness over your deed. Therefore take your provision out of me, for if I pass away I shall not recur to the Day of Resurrection."*

This statement of al-Basri is not a *"hadith al-marfu"[3]* as some people have thought. It is a personal statement of Al-Hasan al-Basri whom Imam 'Ali Zainul 'Abideen describes as, *"This person whose speech resembles the speech of the Prophets"*.

---

[3] A *hadith marfu'* is a *hadith* which could properly be ascribed to the Prophet (SAAS). —Translator.

It is because of this oddity of Time that we find poets and literary men yearning for the return of the days of youth but, alas, that is only a forlorn hope which does not avail anything. One of them says, *"Would that Youth return one day, so that I would narrate to him what (havoc) old-age has wrought!"*

And another poet, imagining how life glides away with its beacons of Night and Day passing by without return and no hope of return, says:

> *"And what is man but a rider on the back of his Life,*
> *On a journey which, with Days and Months, accomplishes he,*
> *Somnolent at Night, awake in the Morning*
> *Each Day and its Night*
> *He's removed from the World, closer to the Sepulchre (a moving grave)."*[4]

3) It is the Most Priceless Possession of Man

As Time possesses these characteristics of flying away quickly, of never returning and of having no substitute, it thus becomes the most precious and most costly thing that man possesses. The preciousness of Time derives from the fact that it is the receptacle and medium of every exertion and activity, every achievement and productivity. For this reason, Time is, in reality, the genuine capital for man, individually and collectively.

Contrary to the widespread proverb, Time is not just money. In reality, it is more expensive than money, gold, diamonds or pearls. It is, as the *shahid* Hasan al-Banna says, life itself. For what is the life of man but the time that he spends from the moment of his birth to the moment of his death?

---

[4] The phrase in parenthesis is not in the original poem. I have added it in, in order to make up the metre. —Translator.

Accordingly, Al-Hasan al-Basri, to quote him once again, says, *"O son of Adam! You are but a bundle of days. As each day passes away, a portion of you vanishes away!"*

Whoever is today ignorant of the value of Time, a moment will slowly but surely dawn on him, when he will realise the worth and preciousness of Time, and the value of exploiting it. However, that moment will be too late. Accordingly, the Qur'an mentions two scenes for man wherein he will regret squandering his time, when regret will not profit him.

Scene One: This is the Hour of Death, when man bids farewell to this World and sets out on his journey to the Hereafter. He will then wish for a temporary postponement, and desire to be tarried for a short while, so that he can put right what he has spoiled, and regain the ground that he has lost. In this respect, the Qur'an says:

"O ye who believe! Let not your wealth nor your children distract you from the remembrance of Allah. If any act thus, surely they are the losers.[5] *And spend something (in charity) out of the substance which We have bestowed on you, before Death should come to any of you and he should say, 'O my Lord! Why did Thou not give me respite for a little while? I should then have given (largely) in charity, and I should have been one of the doers of good."*

(Suratul Munafiqun 63: 9-10)

The reply to this empty wish is a decisive refusal: *"But to no soul will Allah grant respite when the appointed time for it has come; and Allah is well acquainted with (all) that ye do"*.

(Suratul Munafiqun 63: 11)

---

[5] Remembrance of Allah includes every act of service and goodness, which Allah requires of us. If we fail in this, the loss is purely our own, for it stunts our own spiritual growth.

Scene Two: This is in the Hereafter, when each soul shall be paid out in full for its deeds and recompensed for what it has earned. The Guests of Paradise will be admitted therein and the Prisoners of Hellfire will be locked up therein. At this time, the Prisoners of the Hellfire will wish they could be returned once again to this Life of Responsibility, so that they could start anew and work righteousness. This is the most futile demand, for the "Time for Work" is already over, and the "Time of Reward" has already arrived! Allah Ta'ala says, *"But those who reject (Allah)— for them will be the Fire of Hell: no term shall be determined for them, so that they could die, nor shall its chastisement be lightened for them. Thus do We reward every ungrateful one! Therein will they cry aloud (for assistance): "Our Lord! Bring us out: we shall work righteousness, not the (deeds) we used to do!' — 'Did We not give you long enough life so that he that would should receive admonition? And (moreover) the Warner came to you. So taste ye (the fruits of your deeds): for the wrongdoers there is no helper."*

(Suratul Fatir 35: 36-37)

Note how their plea is interrupted with this rebuking enquiry: *"Did We not give you long enough life so that he that would should receive admonition? And (moreover) the Warner came to you."* As such, they cannot find a reply. Allah {SWT} indeed cut off all pretexts when He granted every responsible adult a life long enough to discharge their responsibility, and to take heed when they become heedless about it. This is particularly so in respect of a person who has survived to the age of sixty, for, within the scope of this age, there is sufficient room and ample opportunity for the heedless to awaken, the fugitive to return and the sinner to repent. Thus, in a perfect *hadith* (it is said): *"Allah has cut off the excuse of any person whose death He has postponed until he reaches the age of sixty."* (Reported by Al-Bukhari from Abu Hurairah).

The Concern of the Qur'an and the Sunnah with Time

The Qur'an and the Sunnah have exhibited concern with Time from different angles and in many forms.

Foremost in this respect is their exposition on the importance of Time and the immensity of Allah's blessing inherent in it. Thus the Qur'an, in enumerating the favours of Allah and expounding the significance of Allah's gifts to man, says:

> *"And He has made subject to you the sun and the moon, both diligently pursuing their courses; and the Night and the Day has He (also) made subject to you. And He gives you of all that ye ask Him for. And if ye would count the favours of Allah, never would ye be able to number them."*
>
> (Suratu Ibrahim 14:33-34)

And Allah {SWT} says:

> *"And it is He who made the Night and the Day to follow each other: for such as desire to be mindful or to show their gratitude."*
>
> (Suratul Furqan 25: 62)

In other words, Allah has made the Night to succeed the Day, and the Day the Night so that whoever loses an opportunity in one of them shall have the chance to make it up in the other. In order to expound the importance of Time, Allah swears in the opening of a number of *surahs* revealed before the Hijrah, with portions of Time; for example, the Night, the Day, the Dawn, the Morning Hours and Time (itself). Here are instances:

1. *"By the Night as it conceals (the light); and by the Day as it appears (in glory)."* (Suratul Lail 92: 1-2)

2. *"By the Dawn; and by some Ten Nights."* (Suratul Fajr 89: 1-2)

3. *"By the Morning Hours; and by the Night when it is still."*
                                        (Suratud Dhuha 93: 1-2)

4. *"By the Time; verily man is in a loss."*   (Suratul 'Asr 103: 1-2)

It is well-known among Qur'anic exegetes, and it is within the perception of the Muslims that if Allah swears by anything from among His creation the purpose of this is to draw their attention to that object and awaken them to its revered importance and great influence.

In the wake of the Qur'an comes the Sunnah of the Prophet (SAAS). It emphasises the value of Time and confirms the accountability of man for Time to Allah on the Day of Resurrection, so much so that two principal questions out of the four fundamental questions that man shall be summoned to answer on the Day of Reckoning shall exclusively be on Time. Thus Mu'adh bin Jabal reports that the Prophet (SAAS) says:

"Man shall never be acquitted and discharged on the Day of Resurrection until he has been questioned on four themes:
> *(i) with regard to his Life: in what pursuit did he spend it?*
> *(ii) with regard to his Youth: in what pursuit did he expend it?*
> *(iii) with regard to his Wealth: whence did he earn it and on what did he spend it?*
> *(iv) with regard to his Knowledge; what use did he put it to?"*

(Reported by Al-Bazzar and At-Tabarani with a perfect *isnad*. This text comes from the latter).

And thus shall man, every man, be interrogated on his life, generally, and on his youth, specifically. Yet youth is but a portion of life. However, it has a distinguishing merit which characterises it as the years of exuberance and activity, determination and energy; it is a tenacious watershed perched between two frailties: the frailty of childhood and the frailty of senility, as Allah Ta'ala says:

> *"It is Allah Who created you in a state of weakness, then gave (you) strength after weakness, then, after strength,*

gave (you) weakness and a hoary head".
(Suratu Rum 30: 54)

The Rites and Customs of Islam Emphasise the Value of Time

After the Qur'an and the Sunnah comes the teachings and customs of Islam, which corroborate this great idea and principle: that Time— and every bit of it— is valuable and important. These teachings, bound up with cosmic flow and changes, arouse the consciousness of man and awaken him to the value of Time.

Thus as the Night breaks and removes its veil from the face of the Dawn the muezzin, calling to Allah, stands up pervading the horizon with his call, engaging the ears of Time, inviting the attention of the heedless, awakening the somnolent to rise up and welcome the fresh Morning from Allah. His call is: *"Come to Salah! Come to Prosperity. Salah is better than sleep!"* Thereupon, Commemorative Tongues answer back with the praise of Allah as do Grateful Hearts: *"You have said the truth and you are devout!"* Meanwhile, the Purifying Hands are already at ablution, and the *"Knots of the Shaytan"* are already unfastening[6] from them, as they hurry to the *Fajr Salah.*

And as the midday heat wears on, the sun declines away from the meridian, and people become deeply engrossed in their mundane pursuits and the tiring activities of the day, the muezzin returns with his call for the second time: proclaiming the glory of Allah, acknowledging Allah's exclusive right to worship, attesting to Allah's unity and the messengership of Muhammad (SAAS) and inviting to *Salah* and Prosperity. Thereupon, people disentangle themselves from the claws of their occupations and daily routines so that they can stand, for a few minutes only, in front of their Creator and Sustainer Who regulates and

---

[6] This is an allusion to a sound *hadith* which Imam Al-Bukhari reports in his *As-Sahih*: *"The Shaytan makes three knots at the back of the head of each one of you whilst you are asleep".* See the chapter on "The Daily Way of Life for a Muslim."

14

governs their affairs. During this short moment they put aside their material struggles and preoccupation with earthly pursuits. This is the occasion of the midday *Salah*— *Salatuz Zuhr.*

And when the shadow of each object equals its length, and the sun declines further down the horizon on its course to set, the muezzin calls for the third time inviting to *Salatul 'Asr.*

And at the time when the ball of the sun disappears and its face is screened from the horizon, the muezzin makes yet another call to the *Salah* which marks the end of the Day and the beginning of the Night. That is *Salatul Maghrib.*

And when the twilight disappears and darkness descends, the voice of the Blessed Caller rends the air with its invitation to the *Salah* which seals off the typical day of a Muslim. That is *Salatul 'Isha'.*

In this way, a Muslim starts off his day with *Salah* and ends it with *Salah.* In between the two *Salahs*— at dawn and late night— a Muslim is thus on a continuous and renewable appointment with Allah, as the cosmos moves and changes.

Every week, a Friday makes its debut so that the muezzin makes a fresh call summoning to the weekly congregational *Salah*, which has its own special features and rules. That is the *Friday Salah.*

In addition to these obligatory *Salawāt,* there are non-obligatory *Salawat* during the small hours of the night, during which the Servants of the Beneficent keep vigil before their Lord, prostrate and standing. There is the *Salatud Dhuha* during the early morning hours, and other non-obligatory *Salawāt* at different times of the Day and Night.

At the beginning of each lunar month, a new moon appears. The Muslim welcomes it, glorifying Allah and attesting to His exclusive right to be worshipped as he supplicates his Lord, saying: *"Allah is the Greatest! Allah is the Greatest! Allah is the Greatest! Praise is due to Allah Who has created you and measured out stages for you and made you a sign for all peoples. O Allah! Let it wax on us with Security and Faith, with Peace and Islam, and in harmony with whatever You love and approve of. New moon of blessing and guidance! My Lord and your Lord is Allah"*[7].

And every year in the lunar month of Ramadhan *"when the Gates of the Garden are opened, the Gates of Hellfire are locked up, and the devils are shackled"*,[8] another Caller— this time the Divine Caller— calls out: *"O you who seek to attain the good come here! And O you who aspire to evil limit yourself!"*[9]

That is the occasion when the evildoer repents, the deviant returns, the heedless awakens, and many a fugitive homes in to the side of Allah seeking His pleasure and forgiveness through a befitting observance of the Fast and its Vigil[10] for they have been promised so by His Noble Messenger: *"Whoever observes the Ramadhan Fast, believing (that it is an obligatory duty) and expecting (his reward from Allah), has had his past sins forgiven; and whoever keeps the Ramadhan Vigil, believing (that it is a meritorious voluntary act) and expecting (his reward) has had his past sins forgiven"* [11]

---

[7] Our respected author (may Allah preserve him) is actually quoting the prayer which the Prophet (SAAS) taught the Faithful on the birth of every new moon. (Reported by Ahmad, At-Tirmidhi, At-Tabarani, Ad-Darimi, Ibn Hibban and others).—Translator

[8] Al-Bukhari, Muslim and Ahmad reported from Abu Hurairah that the Prophet (SAAS) said: *"When the lunar month of Ramadhan arrives, the Gates of Paradise are opened, the Gates of Hellfire bolted and the Shayatin chained."*—Translator

[9] Al-Bukhari, Muslim and Ahmad reported from Abu Hurairah that the Prophet (SAAS) said: *"When the lunar month of Ramadhan arrives, the Gates of Paradise are opened, the Gates of Hellfire bolted and the Shayatin chained."*—Translator

[10] The Night Vigil in the fasting month of Ramadhan, which is voluntary but otherwise highly recommended and meritorious, consists of long sessions of *salah* in the course of which the whole Qur'an may be recited over the blessed month. — Translator

[11] These are actually two independent *ahadith*, both reported by Imam Al-Bukhari, otherwise ingeniously joined together here by the author. —Translator

After this spiritual journey in the month of Ramadhan, another journey, which is both physical and spiritual, soon follows in its wake. That is the journey of the Hajj, whose period starts at the very moment Ramadhan ends: *"The Hajj (in) the well-known months.*[12] *If anyone undertakes that duty therein, let there be no obscenity, nor wickedness, nor wrangling in the Hajj. And whatever good ye do Allah knows it. And take a provision (with you) for the journey, but the best of provisions is the right conduct. So fear me, O ye that are wise"*.

(Suratul Baqarah 2: 197)

Some of our predecessors used to describe the Five Daily *Salawāt* as the *"Daily Scales"*, the Friday *Salah* as the *"Weekly Scales"*, the Ramadhan Fast as the *"Yearly Scales"*, and the Hajj as the *"Scales of the Lifetime."*[13] These descriptions express the hope that one's typical day will be sound and flawless. Once the day is over and its success is assured, attention is turned to the success of the week, then to the success of the year, then finally to the success of the lifetime— and that, indeed, is a crowning finish.[14]

Besides the *Salah*, there is the obligation of the *Zakah* which is due every year, and on the occasion of every harvest and gathering in of fruits and green crops: *"And render the dues that are proper on the day that the harvest is gathered"*. With this obligation, a Muslim is kept in constant consciousness of the passage of Time and watchful over its changes, so that he does not postpone the *Zakah* from its due time, i.e. the anniversary or the time of every harvest.

---

[12] The months of Shawwal, Dhul-Qa'ada, and Dhul-Hijjah (up to the 10th or the 13th) are set apart for the rites of Hajj. —Translator

[13] The Muslim should place the deeds of his days, weeks, years and lifetime in the 'scales' to determine his success at various stages of his life. —Translator.

[14] "A crowning finish" may be translated " a fragrant seal," of the Hajj which crowns and seals off the lifetime work of a Muslim. See Qur'an, Suratut Tatfif 83: 26). — Translator.

Duties of a Muslim towards Time

If Time commands all this importance, to the extent that it has, rightfully, been regarded as life itself, then there are indeed many duties incumbent upon a Muslim towards Time. It behoves a Muslim to be aware of these duties, keep them under his constant watch, and translate them from mere theoretical Knowledge to deep-rooted Faith, and thence to Action and Fulfilment.

Parsimony over the Utilisation of Time

The first duty of a Muslim towards his Time is to guard and preserve it, just as he guards and preserves his wealth. He should desire to utilise all of his Time in that which shall profit him in his religion and his personal worldly life, and in that which shall contribute to the welfare and prosperity of his community as well as to its spiritual and material growth.

Our Pious Predecessors (may Allah be pleased with them), were most economical when it came to the issue of their Time, for they, more than anybody else, fully appreciated its value.

Al-Hasan al-Basri[15] says: *"I have lived with a people who were more parsimonious with their Time than you (people) are with your money"*.

As a result of this parsimony with Time, the Forefathers' most profound aspiration was to persistently fill their Time with worthy endeavours, and totally avoid misallocating any portion of it to unworthy pursuits.

---

[15] Imam Al-Hasan bin Yassar al-Basri (21-110A.H/642-728 C.E) was born in Al-Madina and grew up to be one of the learned and eloquent jurists. He used to command and forbid the authorities without fear of blame or criticism. The people that he mentions are the venerable Companions of the Prophet (SAAS), may Allah be pleased with them. — Translator.

The Caliph 'Umar bin Abdul 'Aziz says, *"The Night and the Day work against you, work against them as well."*

The Forefathers would say, *"One of the many hints that one is detested (by Allah) is the wasting of (one's) time."* They would also say, *"Time is a sword; if you do not blunt it, it will sever you."* The Forefathers made increasing efforts to develop themselves on a daily basis, so that each successive day should be better than the day preceding it. Accordingly, one of them said, *"Swindled is the person who does not daily progress, and accursed is the person who daily regresses!"*

They would make every effort to ensure that no day, or part of a day, or moment, however small, passed by without their taking a provision out of it; a provision of useful knowledge, or an excellent deed, or a struggle with (the evil prompting of) the Soul, or doing good to someone, so that their lives would not, as it were, glide away in vain, fizzle out and be brought to naught without their being aware of it.

They would consider it an ingratitude to Allah {SWT}, and a disrespect for Time, that a day should pass away without their deriving some benefit from it, either for themselves or for the society around them, in the form of growth in knowledge, growth in Faith, and growth in excellent deeds.

Ibn Mas'ud (may Allah be pleased with him) says, *"I do not regret anything as much as I regret over a day whose sun has set: in it my appointed time has decreased and (yet) in it my deeds have not increased!"*

Another person says, *"Any day that passes me by and, in it, I have not increased in knowledge that would get me closer to Allah — the Mighty and the Majestic— then I have not been blessed with that day."*

Some scholars have attributed the above citation to the Prophet (peace and blessings of Allah be upon him). However, this attribution has been rejected by Ibn Qayyim in his book *"Miftahu Daris Sa'adah"*. He says, *"It suffices to ascribe it to a companion or to a Tabi'i."*

In the same vein, a poet says, *"If a day passes me by and I have not gained any guidance, nor acquired any knowledge then that (day) is not part of my life."*[16]

A wise man[17] says, *"Whoever expends a day out of his lifetime, not in settling an obligation, or discharging a responsibility, or consolidating a noble reputation, or initiating a praiseworthy deed, or founding a charitable work, or gathering knowledge has indeed misused his Time, and abused himself!"*

Killing Time

If such was the praiseworthy parsimony of our predecessors over Time, and if such was its value and importance, then what we today witness amongst Muslims (the manner in which they dissipate their Time, exceeding the bounds of waste to the sphere of irresponsibility), is a spectacle which breaks the heart and makes one's blood boil in grief and sorrow.

Truly, foolishness in spending Time is more serious than foolishness in spending money, and these irresponsible squanderers of their Time are more deserving indeed of being placed under guardianship[18] than the squanderers of money. For money, when lost, can be replaced; Time, however, once lost, has no substitute.

A popular expression which has become all too familiar, and which one often hears at social gatherings is the expression: *"Killing time"*. As a

---

[16] By this logic it is possible to find teenagers who are (spiritually) in their eighties and likewise people in their eighties who are (spiritually) mere teenagers, or even less than zero! — Translator.

[17] The word *hakim* in the original Arabic could be the name of a person, or be translated as "a wise man" as I have done here. —Translator.

[18] "Guardianship" meaning *Tahjir*: a principle of the *Shari'ah* which, because of immaturity, incompetence or lunacy, denies a person legal freedom in the disposal of his affairs. —Translator.

result of the thought process underlying this phrase, you will see irresponsible users of Time sitting for long hours of the night or day, round a table of backgammon, chess, cards or other games, which may or may not be permissible in the *Shari'ah*. They sit unperturbed, heedless of the Remembrance of Allah, forgetful about the *Salah* and oblivious of their religious and earthly responsibilities. And if you were to ask them about their actions, they would clearly tell you: *"Our intention is no more than to kill time!"*

Little do these poor souls realise that whoever kills his time, has indeed killed himself! Killing time is a form of suicide. It is a terrible crime committed openly and shamelessly in the sight and hearing of all, yet no one is punished for it! But then, how would you go about punishing a person over a crime that they are not aware of and whose gravity they do not appreciate?!

Exploiting Spare-Time

Spare-time is a blessing which many people undervalue, take for granted, and thus fail to utilise properly.

Imam Al-Bukhari reports from the Prophet (SAAS), on the authority of Ibn 'Abbas, that: *"Good health and spare-time are two of the blessings of Allah in respect of which many people are duped"*.

Spare-time is defined as the time during which one is free from the worldly engagements, which normally hinder one from otherwise eminently religious pursuits. This definition does not oppose the many injunctions which encourage man to acquire wealth and earn his livelihood, so long as doing so does not drown him in the deep ocean of earthly life and material pursuits, and so long as it does not prevent him from discharging his obligations to Allah, the Most High.

In the above *hadith*, the Prophet (peace and blessings of Allah be upon him) mentioned 'duping'. Duping primarily takes place in business transactions of buying and selling. However, in our context, as

'Allamah Al-Munawi explains, the adult person has been likened to a trader, and good health and spare-time to business capital which are both necessary for profit and success. This implies that whoever transacts with Allah by observing His commandments shall prosper; and whoever transacts with the *Shaytan* by following him shall lose their business capital.

In another *hadith* the Prophet (peace and blessings of Allah be upon him) says, *"Exploit five (things) before five ..."* and among the five, he mentions, *"Your Spare-time before your Pre-occupation."*[19]

Spare or leisure time is never entirely free or empty. It must necessarily be occupied with either Good or Evil. Whoever does not engage his Soul with the Truth, his Soul will engage him with Falsehood, so blessed are those who fill their spare-time with goodness and benevolence; and damned are those who fill their spare-time with evil and malevolence.

Some pious men say: *"Leisure time is a great blessing. If, therefore, the servant of Allah proves ungrateful for this blessing, by opening upon himself the floodgates of passion, and drifts along in the boat of pleasure, Allah muddles up and removes the serenity that he once had in his heart."*

The author of Al-Hikam says: *"Failure, all failure, lies in your being free from distractions, yet you do not address yourself to Allah; and in unchaining yourself, yet you do not migrate to Him."*

Our pious predecessors would abhor the sight of a person free from all engagements; one who is neither engaged in a religious affair, nor

---

[19] The full text of the *hadith*, reported by Al-Hakim and Al-Bayhaqi on the authority of Ibn 'Abbas, is: *"Exploit five (things) before five: Your life before your death; your good health before your ill health; your spare-time before your preoccupation; your youth before your old-age; your wealth before your poverty."* —Translator.

engaged in an earthly one[20]. This is precisely the time when the boon of leisure metamorphoses into doom for such individuals, regardless of their sex. For this reason, it is said: *"Leisure, for men, induces stupidity; for women, it is erotogenic."* By example, was not the passionate love of the wife of the 'Aziz[21] for Yusuf (A.S.) and her plot to ensnare him all but the result of the leisure that she enjoyed?

The risk posed by leisure assumes greater proportions when it is accompanied by youth — which is distinguished for the intensity of its passion — and money, which empowers man to achieve what he desires. It is in this context that Abul 'Atahiyah says in his poem:

> *"Youth, leisure and money are a catastrophe,*
> *To man indeed what a catastrophe!"*

Another poet says:

> *"Leisure has stirred up events for him,*
> *Yes, the causes of tribulations lie in leisure".*

By 'events which have been stirred up by leisure', the poet means the preoccupations of the heart and its attachment to yearning and daydreaming, which beget naught but unhappy consequences in this life and the next.

Promptness in Doing Good

---

[20] The pious predecessors were taught by the Noble Prophet (SAAS) that: *"The best of you is the one who does not forsake his Life Hereafter for his Earthly Life, nor his Earthly Life for his Life Hereafter, and does not become a burden on other people."* (A sound *hadith* reported by Al-Khateeb from Anas). —Translator.

[21] See Qur'an, Surah Yusuf (12: 23-35) for details of the whole episode. —Translator.

It behoves the Believer, who appreciates the value of Time and its importance, to keep it inundated with good deeds to the extent of his ability. It is not sufficient for him to rise to a good deed with reluctance and lethargy, or to perform part of it and postpone the rest, or to postpone it altogether to another day through sheer laziness. A poet once said:

"The engagements of the day, out of lethargy, I shall not postpone until tomorrow. For, verily, the day of the lethargic is ever on the morrow!"

And from the prayers and remembrances taught by the Prophet (SAAS) to his followers, which a Muslim should recite mornings and evenings, we read:

"O Allah! I seek refuge in You from anxiety and grief, and I seek refuge in You from incompetence and lethargy..."[22]

For that reason, the Noble Qur'an commands the striving, as in a race, towards all that which is good, and competing with one another towards this goal promptly enough before distractions and impediments arrive to make doing so impossible. Allah Ta'ala says:

"To each is a goal to which Allah turns him; then strive together as in a race towards all that is good. Wheresoever ye are, Allah will bring you all together".
(Suratul Baqarah 2: 148)

And commenting on the People of the Book (Jews and Christians) and what was revealed to them, Allah Ta'ala says:

"If Allah had so willed, He would have made you a single people, but (His plan is) to test you in what He has given you: so strive as in a race

---

[22] The full *hadith* has two versions, one reported by both Al-Bukhari and Muslim on the authority of Anas bin Malik, and the other reported by Muslim on the authority of Zayd bin Arqam. —Translator.

in all virtues. The goal of you all is to Allah."
(Suratul Ma'idah 5: 48)

And Allah, Whose affairs are exalted, in arousing our interest in the Paradise and its comforts, says:

"And be quick in the race for forgiveness from your Lord, and for a Paradise whose width is that of the heavens and of the earth, prepared for the righteous."
(Suratu Aal 'Imran 3: 133).

And in another *ayah* (we read):

"Be ye foremost in seeking forgiveness from your Lord and a Paradise the width whereof is as the width of heaven and of the earth."
(Suratul Hadid 57: 21)

Thus Allah commands us to excel with promptness, and race as though in a competition to seek His forgiveness and Paradise; that is to say, to seek the causes of His forgiveness and Paradise, which are Faith, Piety and Good Deeds. Competition and striving to excel one another, in this particular regard, is both desirable and praiseworthy, as the Noble Qur'an states:

"And for this let those aspire, who have aspirations."
(Suratul Mutaffifin 83: 26)

And Allah has showered His praise upon some of His excellent and chosen prophets, by saying:

"Lo! They used to vie one with the other in doing good deeds, and they used to call on Us in yearning and awe and humble themselves before Us."
(Suratul Anbiya 21: 90)

Allah has also commended those who are righteous among the People of the Book, in that:

"They believe in Allah and the Last Day; they enjoin what is right, and forbid what is wrong; and they hasten (in emulation) in (all) good works: they are in the ranks of the righteous."

(Suratu Aal 'Imran 3:114)

In contrast, Allah has castigated the hypocrites by saying:

"When they stand up to worship, they stand without earnestness"

(Suratun Nisa 4: 142)

And by His saying:

"And they come not to worship save lazily and that they offer contributions unwillingly".

(Suratut Taubah 9: 54)

A further argument in support of this proposition is that the Prophet (SAAS) used to command his followers to hasten in doing good works before the advent of impediments and civil strifes. He would say: *"Hasten in doing good deeds ahead of some seven calamities! Are you waiting for anything except (1) a poverty that will make you forget, or (2) a prosperity that will make you transgress, or (3) a sickness that will incapacitate, or (4) an old-age that will confuse, or (5) a sudden death, or (6) the Dajjal (Anti-Christ): lo! He is a hidden evil that is being awaited, or (7) the Hour: behold! The Hour is most grievous, most bitter!*[23]

And the Prophet (SAAS), in yet another good *hadith* reported by At-Tirmidhi, says: *"He who fears (being late) sets out at nightfall, and he who sets out at nightfall, shall reach his destination. Look! The merchandise of Allah is expensive. Look! The merchandise of Allah is Paradise"*[24]

---

[23] Reported by At-Tirmidhi on the authority of Abu Hurairah.

[24] Paradise is not for the lazy, nor for those who delay in doing good deeds. He who aspires to Paradise has a very long distance to cover and must set out early to reach his cherished destination. Paradise is a precious article for sale by Allah, so its price must

Taking Lessons from the Passage of Time

It behoves a Believer to take personal lessons from the passage of days and nights. The passing of Time wears out the new, brings what is remote nearer, rolls up lifetimes, makes the young old, and annihilates the old. As the poet, in olden times once said:

> *"The passing of time has produced*
> *Grey hair in the young, decay in the aged;*
> *As the Night wears out its Day,*
> *Soon enough comes a man's doomsday."*

The passing of Time, manifested in the alternation of Day and Night, should not float away from a Believer without his taking a lesson from it. For instance, in the course of each day, each hour, and each moment, innumerable events take place in life and in the cosmos. On Earth, a seed germinates, a plant flowers, a flower bears fruit, a fruit is plucked and a crop soon becomes dry stubble scattered by the winds. A foetus comes into being, a child is born, a baby grows into adolescence, a youth matures into adulthood, an adult ages into senility, and an old person dies away.[25] In addition to these earthly phenomena, there are numerous changes taking place in the celestial sphere, unseen but no less potent.

During the course of these continual changes, we pass through states of ease and adversity, prosperity and poverty, health and ill-health, happiness and sorrow, comfort and discomfort, fortune and misfortune. In all these there are signs for those who are intelligent, messages for those with an understanding heart, and lessons for those with vision. As for those who lack the thought processes of the intelligent, the

---

be paid. Its price is faith, sacrifice, and strenuous and prompt effort in doing all that which is good and virtuous. (See Qur'an Suratut Taubah 9: 111) —Translator.

[25] Compare this with the Latin *"Tempus edax rerum"* (Time is the consumer of all things), and Shakespeare's *"Nothing 'gainst Time's scythe can make defence."*— Translator.

perception of men of understanding, and the vision of the genius, the flow of Time (reflected in the alternation of Night and Day) shall never profit them. Allah Ta'ala says:

"Behold! In the creation of the heavens and the earth, and the alternation of Night and Day,— there are indeed signs for men of understanding."

(Suratu Aal 'Imran 3: 190)

And Allah, exalted are His affairs, says:

"It is Allah Who alternates the Night and the Day: verily in these things is an instructive example for those who have vision!"

(Suratun Noor 24: 44)

Organising Time

It behoves a Believer to organise his time in respect of his obligatory and other duties, both religious and mundane, so that one does not dominate the other, the unimportant does not overshadow the important, the important does not prevail over the more important, and the timeless does not take precedence over the time-specific. Thus, an urgent duty should be expeditiously performed, and a less urgent one deferred to a later time; and a duty that has a prescribed time, should be consummated within its specified time.

The Prophet (peace and blessings of Allah be upon him) has narrated this quotation from the Books of Ibrahim: *"It behoves an intelligent man —in so far as he behaves rationally— to have four time periods: a period in which he converses with his Lord; a period in which he cross - examines himself; a period in which he reflects over the artistry of*

Allah, the Almighty, the Exalted; a period which he devotes to his needs for food and drink. "[26]

Of all people, those who are in greater need to apportion and organise their time, are those who are charged with public responsibilities. This is so, because of the competing burdens they carry, so much so that they feel there are more obligations than they have time for.

It is part of organising time to set a portion of it for rest and refreshment. The soul tires of long periods of application, and the heart grows weary, just as the body grows weary. A modest amount of amusement and lawful pastime is, therefore, necessary in life, as 'Ali (may Allah be pleased with him) says: *"Give the heart an hour of rest after an hour of exertion, for the heart, if forced, gets blindfolded."*

It does not befit a Muslim to overburden himself with work to the extent that it violates the rights of his soul, the rights of his family, and the rights of his society. This applies even if such exertion is in the worship of Allah, be it by way of fasting, *Salah*, sacrifice, or abstinence.

It is for this reason that the Prophet (SAAS), when he saw his Companions ever congregating behind him for the night vigil, said to them: *"Take from work what you can, for verily Allah does not stop (rewarding you) until you get fed up (in worshipping Him); and verily the most beloved of works to Allah is that which is most constant even if it is meagre"*[27]

In another instance he said: *"Verily this Religion (of Islam) is very easy. No one ever challenges this Religion but it overcomes him. So be*

---

[26] Reported by Ibn Hibban in his collection of sound *ahadith* in a long *hadith* narrated by Abu Dharr.

[27] Reported by the Two Sheikhs (Al-Bukhari and Muslim) from the *hadith* of 'A'isha.

moderate, and try to approach perfection, and receive the glad tidings."[28]

And he advises the person who excessively reads the Qur'an, stands up in *Salah* (in the nights) and fasts (during the day), to be moderate and balanced, saying: *"Indeed your body has a right over you, your family has a right over you, and your wife has a right over you".*[29]

And to those others who exceeded the limits of piety and abstinence, he said: *"I am more devout to Allah than you are and I am more conscious of my duty to Him than you are. Yet I stand up in Salah at night and sleep; and I fast and I cease to fast; and I marry women. So whoever turns away from my practice he is not of me".*[30]

This, therefore, is the *sunnah* (i.e. constant practice) of the Prophet (SAAS), and this is his method: an open, plain, easy road of moderation and observance of balance between spiritualism and materialism; an equilibrium between the requirement of the self and the right of the Lord.

Islam, therefore, sees nothing wrong or objectionable in a man setting aside a portion of his time for the refreshment of his soul, employing in the process all that is good and lawful from the pleasures and beautiful things of life, and its amusements and games.

For this reason, when the Messenger (SAAS) heard Hanzalah (one of his Companions) accusing himself of hypocrisy, because his comportment

---

[28] Reported by Al-Bukhari and An-Nasa'i from Abu Hurairah. Its meaning, as explained by Al-Munawi in *At-Taysir*, is that anyone who exaggerates in worship and defies the ease of this Religion, as the monk does, fails and is overcome. *'So be moderate...'* means endeavour to achieve the perfect balance: no exaggeration, no neglect. *'And try to approach perfection...'* means if you cannot be perfect, then strive so that you approach perfection. *'And receive the glad tidings...'* that Allah will reward you for regular deeds even if meagre.

[29] Reported by Al-Bukhari.

[30] Reported by Al-Bukhari.

30

changes when he is at home in the company of members of his family, from his comportment when he is with the Messenger of Allah, he (SAAS) said to him: *"If you were to remain in the condition that you find yourselves in when you are with me and in constant remembrance of Allah, the angels would certainly shake hands with you in your beds and on your streets. However, O Hanzalah, there is an hour (for worship) and an hour (for attending to the needs of man).*

This, therefore, is the embodiment of the affairs or lifestyle of a Muslim: an hour for this and an hour for that. In other words, an hour for his Lord, and an hour for his heart, as the saying goes.

Al-Asma'i has reported that he once saw a lady in the village. In her hand she held a string of prayer beads[31], and at the same time she was busy applying cosmetics to herself. He said: *'I said to her, "What has this got to do with that?"'* (By this, he was implying that she could not conceivably have been devout and at the same time concerned with beauty and fashion). Thereupon the lady began to say:

"For Allah there's a side of me which I dare neglect not,
And amusement and idle moments do have, in me, a soft spot!"

Al-Asma'i said, *'I then understood that she was indeed a virtuous married lady, beautifying herself for her husband!'*

---

[31] It is more rewarding to use one's fingers than a string of beads to keep count of one's recitals, for that was the practice and recommendation of the Prophet (SAAS). As for using stones, seeds, etc., there were some Companions, including Abu Hurairah, who used to do that. It has also been reported that the Prophet (SAAS) saw one of his wives keeping count using stones, and he confirmed her practice. However, the use of a string of beads has been disapproved by some scholars, whilst others have not disapproved of its use. Provided one's intention is good, such use is good. However, holding the string of beads without a devotional purpose, or displaying it to the public view in order to make a show, is at the very least greatly disapproved of. (See Imam Ibn Qayyim's *Al-Wabilus Sayyib* and vol. 22 of Imam Ibn Taymiyyah's *Majmu'ul Fatawa*). – Translator.

There is an Appropriate Work for Each Occasion

It behoves a believer to know the type of work called for by each occasion— the work of the heart, or of the tongue, or of the body— so that he may pursue it and strive to accomplish it in its appointed time and merit the acceptance of Allah.

Abu Bakr, in his counsel to 'Umar when he was making him a caliph, said: *"You should know that there is a duty due to Allah in the day which He does not accept at night, and a duty at night which He does not accept in the day"*.[32]

It is not important then for a person to do anything at any time. Rather, what is important, is for him to do the *right* thing at the *right* time. It is for this reason that Allah {SWT} sets out prescribed times for a great number of acts of worship and religious obligations, which should be strictly adhered to; neither hastening nor postponement of performance is permissible. In this way, Allah {SWT} teaches us that a duty performed before, or after its appointed time, shall not be accepted. Allah (be He glorified) says, in the case of *Salah*:

"Verily Salah has been enjoined on Believers at stated times."
(Suratun Nisa 4: 103)

And in the case of the Ramadhan fast, He says:

"So every one of you who is present (at his home) during that month should spend it in fasting."
(Suratul Baqara 2: 185)

And with regards to the Hajj:

"The Hajj is (in) the well-known months."
(Suratul Baqara 2: 197)

---

[32] Abu Bakr's counsel to 'Umar continues: *"And know that Allah does not accept supererogatory performance until the obligatory one has been performed."*

And with regards to the *Zakah*:

> *"And pay the due thereof upon the harvest day."*
> (Suratul An'am 6: 141)

Likewise, the works of the heart[33] and the works of the tongue must necessarily take place within their appointed time and specified period.

A learned gentleman says: *"Every person has but four moments... (moments of) comfort, affliction, pious deed and sin. And in each of these moments there is a requisite share of servitude due to Allah from you, which has been made obligatory on you by virtue of His Lordship (Rububiyyah).*

"So, at the moment of performing a pious deed, a person should display his servitude to Allah through his appreciation and consciousness of Allah's favour on him, in that Allah has guided him to the pious deed and given him the chance to perform it.

"And in a moment of comfort, a person should display his servitude to Allah through gratitude, which is the delight taken by the heart over what Allah has wrought.

"And if a person is engaged in committing an evil deed, the way he should display his servitude to Allah is through repentance and seeking forgiveness.

"And if a person is in a moment of affliction, the way he should display his servitude to Allah is through acceptance and patience. By acceptance we mean to accept the fact that this is from Allah; and by patience we mean the steadfastness of the heart in its faith in the Lord."

---

[33] The works of the heart, which are internal and hence invisible, are what determine the external, visible activities of the body and its limbs. This relationship is perhaps best illustrated in the *ayah*: *"(Allah) knows the treachery of the eyes, and all that the hearts conceal."* (Qur'an Suratu Ghafir 40: 19). —Translator.

What this learned gentleman says is an interpretation of what the Qur'an and the Sunnah declare.

Thus in respect of the moment of performing a pious deed, Allah {SWT} declares:

> *"Say, 'In the Bounty of Allah, and in His mercy,— in that let them rejoice': that is better than the (wealth) they hoard."*
>
> (Suratu Yunus 10: 58)

And in respect of the moment of comfort, Allah {SWT} says:

> *"Eat of the sustenance (provided) by your Lord, and be grateful to Him: a territory fair and happy and a Lord Oft-forgiving."*
>
> (Suratus Saba 34: 15)

And in respect of the moment of committing an evil deed, Allah {SWT} declares:

> *'Say, "O My servants who have transgressed against their souls! Despair not of the mercy of Allah: for Allah forgives all sins."*
>
> (Suratuz Zumar 39: 53)

And in respect of the moment of affliction, He says:

> *"Be sure We shall test you with something of fear and hunger, and some loss in wealth, lives and the fruits (of your toil), but give tidings to those who patiently persevere,— who, when afflicted with a calamity, say: 'Lo! To Allah we belong and lo! Unto Him we are returning."*
>
> (Suratul Baqara 2: 155-156)

This is as far as the Qur'an is concerned. As for the Sunnah, it is thus reported in Sahih Muslim, from the Prophet (peace and blessings of Allah be upon him): *"Take wonder at the affair of a Believer. All his affairs are good for him, and it is not so for anybody except the Believer. If a happy event visits him he is grateful; so it will be good for him. And if a calamity befalls him he is patient; so it will be good for him."*

Seizing Propitious Moments

It behoves a Muslim who is interested in competing in good deeds to seize upon the various times which Allah has distinguished with certain spiritual characteristics, which exalt them above other times. It has been reported in a *hadith*: *"Behold! There are certain fragrant (i.e. exalted) moments to your Lord in your days. So turn your attention to them."*[34]

To designate and reserve certain periods of time for certain special purposes, is the exclusive affair of Allah: He chooses for His special mercy whom He will and what He will.

So just as Allah has exalted some individuals above others, some species above others, and some places above others, likewise He has exalted some periods of time above others: *"Thy Lord does create and choose as He pleases: the choice is not theirs."* (Suratul Qasas 28: 68)

So from the nocturnal period, Allah has exalted the hours of the dawn; that is to say, the last third of the night, when He manifests Himself to His servants, every night, and descends to them in a manner that befits His Majesty, and calls out:

"Is there anyone who seeks forgiveness, so that I shall forgive him? Is there anyone who seeks repentance, so that I shall accept his repentance? Any one who supplicates? Any one who calls out?"
So it will be until the morning twilight appears.[35]

---

[34] Reported by At-Tabarani from the *hadith* narrated by Muhammad bin Maslamah. Sheikh al-Albani has mentioned it in the weak *ahadith* of *al-Jami' us-Saghir*. (There are minor differences between the text here and that in *al-Jami' us-Saghir*). — Translator.

[35] Reported by Ahmad and Muslim from both Abu Saeed and Abu Hurairah.

For this reason, Allah describes the pious doers of good in this way:

"As to the pious, they will be in the midst of Gardens and Springs; taking joy in the things which their Lord gives them, because, before then, they have done good deeds; they were in the habit of sleeping but little by night; and in the hours of early dawn, they (were found) praying for forgiveness."

(Suratuz Zariyat 51: 15-18)

And the Prophet (peace and blessings of Allah be upon him) says: *"The closest that the Lord gets to His servant, is in the middle of the last part of the night.*[36] *Therefore, if you can endeavour to be among those who remember Allah in that hour, do so."*[37]

From the weekdays, Allah has exalted Friday, which is the Weekly Festival Day for the Muslims. It is the day in which they hold the Obligatory Congregational Worship, the day of reunion, and the day in which falls the hour of fulfilment, which no Muslim encounters, supplicating Allah for some good, except he has his prayer fulfilled.[38]

It has been perfectly established in the *hadith* that whoever hastens in the morning to the Friday Congregational Worship during the first hour, will be (in reward) like the person who has sacrificed a camel; and whoever proceeds in the second hour— that is to say the second shift—

---

[36] Consider this *hadith* along with the *hadith* reported by Muslim, Abu Dawud and An-Nasa'i from Abu Hurairah in which the Prophet (SAAS) says: *"The closest the servant (of Allah) gets to (the mercy of) his Lord is while he prostrates to Him. Therefore, supplicate a lot."*— Translator.

[37] Reported by At-Tirmidhi from 'Amr bin 'Abasah.

[38] Imam Ibn Qayyim (RA), in his work entitled *Zaadul Ma'ad fiy Hadyi Khairil 'Ibad,* cites over thirty characteristics of the day. And from the *hadith* of 'Abdullah bin Salaam, reported by Ibn Majah, the Prophet (SAAS) has indicated that the hour of fulfilment *"is a portion of"* and falls within *"the last hours"* of Friday evening. — Translator.

he will be like the person who has sacrificed a cow, then like the person who sacrificed a sheep, then a hen, then an egg, thence the angels close up their registers as the imam mounts the pulpit for the sermon.

From the days of the year, Allah the Most High has exalted the first ten days of Dhul Hijjah (the twelfth month of the Islamic calendar);[39] and the most exalted of them is the Day of 'Arafah, which is also, without exception, the most exalted day of the year. It has been reported in a *hadith* traceable to the Prophet (SAAS), from Ibn 'Abbas that:

'"There is not, of all days, a day in which deeds are most loved by Allah than these days, i.e. the first ten days of Dhul Hijjah." They (Companions) said, "Not even Jihad (utmost striving) in the cause of Allah?" He said, "Not even Jihad in the cause of Allah, except if a man goes out with his life and property and he does not return with either of them." ' (Reported by Al-Bukhari).

From the months, Allah has exalted the month of Ramadhan, in which the Qur'an was sent down as a guide to mankind, with clear proofs of the Guidance and the Criterion (of right and wrong). In it, fasting has been made obligatory, the Night Vigil supererogatory, and increase in good deeds recommended. It is really the season of the Believers, the 'shop floor' of the righteous, and the 'race track' of the competitors in good deeds.

The Forefathers used to long for this month and await it impatiently, saying (when it arrived): *"Welcome to the Spiritual Cleanser."* They hoped, in the course of it, to cleanse themselves from the impurities of

---

[39] Some authorities consider the first ten days of Dhul Hijjah as the best days of the year; better than the last ten days of Ramadhan because in both months fasting, *salah*, charity, etc. have been enjoined but Dhul Hijjah is further distinguished with the activities of the Hajj.

their imperfections, and purify themselves from the filth of their bestialities,[40] for Allah loves those who purify themselves.

From 'Ubadah bin as-Samit, it is narrated that the Prophet (SAAS), on the arrival of the month of Ramadhan, once said:

"Ramadhan, a month of blessing, has come to you. Allah enshrouds you in it: so He sends down (His) Mercy, mitigates sins and answers prayers. Allah observes how you compete with one another to win His pleasure; He takes pride in and challenges His angels with you. So think well of Allah about yourselves. Lo! The wretched of the Hereafter is the one who has been denied the Mercy of Allah— the Mighty, the Exalted— in this month."

The whole of Ramadhan is an important month. However, the most important part of it is the last third; that is to say, its last ten days. Their superlative importance derives from two factors:

Firstly, they represent the concluding days of the month, and deeds are exclusively judged by their conclusions.[41] It was thus part of a transmitted supplication: *"O Allah! Make the end of my life the best part of it, the best part of my work its conclusion and the best of my days the day I meet you."*[42]

---

[40] I have translated the Arabic *dhunub* (sing. *dhanb*) as bestialities. *Dhanb* (sin, crime, misdeed) derives from *dhanab,* meaning 'tail' —a distinctive feature of beasts—and connotes that when a person sins he has, as it were, abandoned his humanity, developed a tail and thus taken after the beasts. —Translator.

[41] *"Deeds are exclusively judged by their conclusions and lifetimes by their final moments."* A lifetime of devotion is nullified by an act of apostasy, whilst a long, wicked lifetime of *kufr* is overlooked by Allah the moment the sinner repents and returns to Him. In this there is a powerful warning to the devout: never lapse into evil; and to the evildoer: never despair of the mercy of Allah. —Translator.

[42] Reported by Ibn us-Sunni from Anas (RAA). Sheikh Abdul Qadir al-Arna'ut, in An-Nawawi's *al-Adhkar,* says it is a weak *hadith.* —Translator.

Secondly, they represent the time when the Night of Power is expected, the Night which Allah makes better than one thousand months, and the Night in respect of whose excellence He sent down a *surah* from His Book:

"We have indeed sent down this (Message) in the Night of Power. And what will explain to thee what the Night of Power is? The Night of Power is better than a thousand months. The angels and the Spirit descend therein, by the permission of their Lord, with all decrees. (That Night) is Peace until the rising of the dawn."

(Suratul Qadr 97: 1-5)

This Night is definitely in the month of Ramadhan, as the Qur'an has established that Ramadhan is the month in which the Qur'an was sent down.[43] Hence, the Night of Power is a night in this month. And a number of *ahadith* have come down to us instructing us to seek the Night of Power in the last ten days of Ramadhan.

On the arrival of the last ten days of Ramadhan, the Messenger of Allah (SAAS) would gird himself,[44] keep awake in worship for whole nights and urge members of his family to do the same. Furthermore, he used to reserve these days for the *I'tikaf* (retreat to the mosque for devotion and worship).

Besides Ramadhan, Allah has also exalted other months. These are the Sacred Months, which comprise Rajab, Dhul Qa'adah, Dhul Hijjah and Muharram. Allah {SWT} says:

"The number of months in the sight of Allah is twelve months (in a year) — so ordained by Him the day He created the heavens and the

---

[43] Refer to Qur'an (2:185), (44:3) and (97:1). —Translator.

[44] The expression "would gird himself" used by 'A'isha (RAA) in this *hadith*, which has been reported by both Al-Bukhari and Muslim, has, according to an-Nawawi, two connotations: firstly, that he would brace his mind for the extra devotion, and secondly, he would keep away from his wives. —Translator.

earth; of them four are sacred: that is the right religion. So wrong not yourselves in them."

(Suratut Taubah 9: 36)

To wrong oneself is forbidden in every month. However, to wrong oneself in the Sacred Months, is a more grievous error.

The Daily Way of Life for a Muslim

It behoves a Muslim, if he desires to be blessed in his lifetime, to live in accordance with the daily way of life in Islam. This way of life requires that he wakes up early and goes to bed early.

The day of a Muslim starts with the coming of the dawn or, at least, before sunrise. In this way, he experiences the pure, immaculate morning freshness before it is sullied by the breath of sinners, who do not awake from their slumber except at forenoon.

Thus, a Muslim welcomes his day from its very early hours, which the Messenger prays to Allah to bless for his community, when he says: *"O Allah! Bless for my community its early (morning) hours."*[45]

An epidemic which has plagued the Muslims, is that they have reversed the structure of their way of life. As a result, they stay up late at night, then sleep until they miss the opportunity to observe (in its time) the Dawn *Salah*. One of the predecessors has said: *" I wonder at the person who observes the Dawn Salah after sunrise: how could he prosper!"*

Al-Bukhari has reported from Abu Hurairah that the Prophet (SAAS) said: *"The Shaytan ties three knots on the back of the head of everyone of you the moment he sleeps. On each knot he stamps: 'You have a long*

---

[45] Reported by Ahmad, the authors of As-Sunan, Ibn Hibban and al-Hakim from Sakhr bin Wada'ah al-Ghamidi; Ibn Majah from Ibn 'Umar; and At-Tabarani from a number of Companions.

*night, therefore sleep on!' Now if the person wakes up and remembers
Allah a knot unties; then if he performs ablution a second knot unties;
then if he performs the Salah the third knot unties. So he will enter
upon that morning with zeal and delight; otherwise, he will enter upon
that morning depressed and sluggish."*

There could not be a greater distinction between, on the one hand, a
Muslim from whom all the knots of the *Shaytan* have been untied and
who then begins his day with remembrance of Allah, ritual purification
and *Salah* (worship), and sets out to the battle ground of life with zeal,
delight and an open heart; and, on the other hand, a man on whose head
the knots of the *Shaytan* persist, who then begins the morning by
sleeping into the forenoon — heavy, sluggish, retarded and depressed!

A Muslim typically starts his day with obedience to Allah, observing
his supererogatory and obligatory worship, reciting as much as may be
easy for him of the various morning invocations of Allah (*dhikr*) which
have been transmitted from the Messenger of Allah (SAAS), such as:

(1) *"We have entered upon the morning and so has Sovereignty—all
belonging to Allah. Praise be to Allah, there is no deity save Allah. He
is alone, without a partner to Him. To Him belongs the Sovereignty
and to Him belongs the Praise and He has power over all things. My
Lord! I beg You for the good which is in this night and the good which
follows thereafter; and I seek refuge in You from the evil which is in this
night and the evil which follows thereafter. My Lord! I seek refuge in
You from sloth, and from the evil of old-age. My Lord! I seek refuge in
You from the torment of the Hellfire and the torment of the grave."*

(2) *O Allah! With Your help and permission do we enter upon the
morning, and with Your help and permission do we enter upon the
evening. With Your help and permission do we live and with Your help
and permission do we die; and unto You shall be the resurrection."*[46]

---

[46] Reported by Imam At-Tirmidhi from Abu Hurairah who said: *"The Prophet (SAAS)
used to instruct his Companions. He would say, "If any one of you enters upon the
morning then let him say..."* and he narrated the invocation. —Translator.

(3) *"O Allah! Whatever grace I or any one of Your creatures may find this morning is from You alone, You have no partner. Therefore, all praise and thanksgiving belong to You."*[47]

(4) *"O Allah! I have entered upon the morning in grace, good health and protection from You. Therefore, complete Your grace on me, and Your (bestowal of) good health and protection in this life and the next".*[48]

Thereafter, he will read what Allah wills for him from His Noble Book, with humility, contemplation and effort to understand its meanings, in accordance with what Allah {SWT} Himself says:

"(This is) a book which We have sent down unto thee, full of blessings, that they may meditate on its signs, and that men of understanding may receive admonition.

(Suratu Sād 38: 29)

Next, he will take his moderate breakfast, and then turn his attention to his daily pursuits, making an effort to plan his livelihood and seek his sustenance. He strives to occupy himself with any permissible pursuit, no matter how wealthy and prosperous he may be, even if such engagement involves no more than supervision and control, for unattended wealth is vulnerable to theft.

To this end, Islam forbids interest, as it is an arrangement wherein money inevitably yields money without the money-lender doing any work, and without his sharing any risks or losses. Rather, he sits comfortably in his high chair, absolutely certain that his money will bring him a rate of return of so much per cent, without his undertaking any responsibility whatsoever. This, to be sure, is contrary to the view of Islam about man, which is that man has been created so that he will toil and husband the earth:

---

[47] Reported by Abu Dawud from 'Abdullah bin Gannam (RAA). —Translator.

[48] Reported by Ibn As-Sunni from Ibn 'Abbas (RAA). —Translator.

"It is He (Allah) Who has produced you from the earth and made you husband it."

(Suratu Hud 11: 61)

Just as an individual receives value from life, it is incumbent upon him to give value to it; and just as he consumes from it, it behoves him to produce for it. He should not be idle and unemployed, eating and not working, even if it be on the pretext of consecrating himself to the worship of Allah, for there is no monasticism in Islam.

Imam al-Baihaqi has reported from 'Abdullah bin Az-Zubair who says: *"The most evil thing in the world is unemployment."* Allamah Al-Munawi, in his *"Faidul Qadir"*, has commented on this, saying: *"This is so because if a man is out of work, he engages his mind with any lawful pursuit that may help him spiritually and psychologically. Thus outwardly, he appears idle, yet his mind is engaged. No; the Shaytan builds up his nest in his mind, lays his eggs and hatches them, and therein they multiply faster than would bacteria. So, whoever does not benefit mankind with a trade which he practises, remains a mere consumer of their productive effort, and (thus) makes their resources the more scarce, has no use in communal life, except rocking the boat and escalating (demand and) prices."*

For this reason, whenever he saw a prominent person, the Caliph 'Umar would ask him: *"Do you have a trade?"* If he replied in the negative, he would drop in 'Umar's estimation of him. An indicator of the ignominy and repugnance of this consumer - idler lifestyle is to be found in the rebuke (by the *Shari'ah*) of the person who consumes his own[49] wealth wastefully and in haste. If such a person has been reproached, what more of the person who consumes the wealth of others and neither compensates them, nor offers them any substitute?

---

[49] I do not find such a rebuke except in respect of a trustee who wastefully and in haste consumes the wealth entrusted to him of minor orphans against their growing up (Qur'an 4:6). This, however, does not detract anything from the force and logic of the author's argument. —Translator.

A Muslim's earthly pursuits are counted as acts of worship and jihad, so long as such is his intention and he carries out the pursuit excellently and faithfully, with full remembrance of Allah.

Excellence in performance is a religious duty upon the Muslim, as the Prophet (Peace and Blessings of Allah be upon him) says: *"Verily Allah has enjoined excellent performance upon everything."*

This is a *hadith* reported by Muslim. In another *hadith* reported by Al-Baihaqi, Abu Ya'ala and Ibn Asakir from 'A'isha, the Prophet (SAAS) says: *"Verily Allah loves if one of you performs a deed that he should perfect it."*

One of the daily obligations which it is not permissible for a Muslim to either forget or neglect, is his obligation of service towards the society, assisting its individual members to accomplish their needs, and facilitating their affairs.

The Two Sheikhs have reported from Abu Musa, from the Prophet (Peace and Blessings of Allah be upon him) who said: *"'Upon every Muslim there is (an obligation of) charity."* The Companions said, "O Messenger of Allah! What then happens if he does not have the wherewithal?" He said, "He should do some (manual) work, so that he benefits himself and gives out (his surplus in) charity." They said, "What if he cannot, or if he does not work?" He said, "He should assist someone in dire need." They said, "And if he did not?" He said, "Then let him command what is (in conscience and in law) good." They said, "And if he did not?" He said, "Then let him eschew evil, that indeed is a charity."'*

This charity, or social levy, is an obligation each day upon every Muslim. Furthermore, it has been most reliably reported that this charitable duty is incumbent upon every single limb, or organ, of a Muslim each day. With such an injunction a Muslim turns out to be a spring from which flows goodness, welfare and peace to whoever and whatever is around him.

It has been reported in both Muslim and Al-Bukhari from Abu Hurairah, who said: 'The Messenger of Allah (SAAS) says, *"Charity is due from every joint of each person every day the sun rises: if you justly reconcile between any two (disputing parties), it is charity; if you help a man with his mount so that you lift him up onto it or you hoist up to him his baggage, it is charity; a good word is charity; every step you take to (the place of) Salah, is charity; if you remove harmful things from the pathway, it is charity."*[50]

What has here been translated as "joints" refers to bones, joints and bodily organs, as corroborated by other *ahadith*. These are a favour upon man from Allah, the One, Who created him, then fashioned him in due proportion, then gave him a just bias, and assembled him in the best form.[51] It is, therefore, incumbent upon man to show gratitude to Allah {SWT} for these endowments, by employing them in compliance with His commands, and in the service and welfare of His servants in all possible ways.

By noon, the call to *Zuhr* is made, whereupon the Muslim hastens to perform his *Salah*, striving his utmost to render it as soon as it has become due, in congregation if possible. This is because the good pleasure of Allah is to be found in offering the *Salah* at the earliest time its obligation falls due. Allah {SWT} has enjoined striving, as in a race, in all good works; and the Messenger, peace and blessings of Allah be upon him, once intended to set fire to the houses of those people who stayed away from the *Salah* in congregation.[52] Congregational worship

---

[50] "...harmful things from the pathway..." These could literally be obstacles in the road, or obstacles to one's physical and spiritual well-being. Intoxicants, *haram* food, obscene literature, films and godless theories are all examples of harmful things along the spiritual path, which must, in charity to humanity, be removed. —Translator.

[51] See explanation of Surah 82: 7-8. —Translator.

[52] Reported by the Two Sheikhs from Abu Hurairah.—Translator.

is, in law, twenty-seven times better than worshipping alone, particularly if such congregational worship takes place in the mosque.[53]

At midday, a Muslim takes his meal. He moderately eats from the good things Allah has provided, neither so much that he becomes stuffed, nor so little that it is not sufficient, as Allah {SWT} says:

'O children of Adam! Wear your beautiful apparel at every time and place of worship; and eat, but waste not by excess, for Allah loves not the wasters. Say: "Who has forbidden the beautiful (gifts) of Allah, which he has produced for His servants, and the things, clean and pure, (which He has provided) for sustenance?"'

(Suratul A'araf 7: 7-8)

In tropical regions, especially during the summer, some people may take an afternoon siesta. In this way, they seek to assist themselves for the night vigil and the early morning rise. It is this that the Qur'an alludes to when it says: *"...and the while ye doff your clothes for the noonday heat..."* (Suratun Noor 24: 58)

When the time of *'Asr* comes, and the muezzin invites to it saying: *"Come to Salah"*, the Muslim wakes up from his siesta, or gives up his work, as the case may be, and hastens to this *Salah*, which is regarded as the *"Middle Salah"*[54] for the day. It is not permissible for a Muslim to be distracted from it by any form of trade, commerce or pastime. Hence, the Faithful, as Allah has described them in His Book, are *"men whom neither trade nor business can divert from the remembrance of Allah, nor from regular Salah, nor from paying Zakah; who fear a Day when hearts and eyes will be turned about."* (Suratun Noor 24: 37)

---

[53] Women have the right to attend congregational *salah* in the mosques, but it is more meritorious for them to perform the *salah* in their homes. (See *Sahih Ibn Khuzaimah, vol.3*). – Translator.

[54] For an explanation of the phrase *"Middle Salah"*, see 'Abdullah Yusuf 'Ali's commentary on Qur'an 2: 238). —Translator.

It is not befitting for a Muslim to trivialise and delay the *'Asr Salah* until its time is almost up, for that is the *Salah* of hypocrites, as the Prophet (SAAS) said: *"That is the Salah of a hypocrite! That is the Salah of a hypocrite! That is the Salah of a hypocrite: he keeps an eye on the disk of the sun until it declines between the two horns of the Shaytan when, (like a bird), he pecks its four Raka'at not remembering Allah in the process except little."* (Reported by Muslim)

And as soon as the sun sets, a Muslim hurries to perform *Maghrib*, the sunset *Salah*, at its prime time, in the knowledge that its time is particularly limited. When he has discharged this obligation, he then recites as much as may be easy for him from the transmitted evening memorials of Allah (dhikr), for example: *"O Allah! This is the (hour of the) advent of Your night, and the retreat of Your day and the petitions of Your supplicants. Do Thou then forgive me!"* [55]

One can also repeat the morning supplications, but in place of the phrase: *"We have entered upon the morning,"* one should substitute the phrase: *"We have entered upon the evening."*

A Muslim then takes his supper, without being wasteful or ascetic. He then performs his *'Isha' Salah* as well as its accompanying voluntary *Raka'at*. He may delay the *Witr*, if he is accustomed to waking up later in the night; otherwise, he should perform it before he sleeps.

A Muslim may delay taking his supper until after the *'Isha' Salah*. However, if supper is ready at the time of *'Isha'* he should give priority to the former, as instructed in the *hadith*.[56] The rationale behind this is

---

[55] Reported by Abu Dawud and At-Tirmidhi from Umm Salamah who said: *"The Messenger of Allah (SAAS) taught me that I should say at the call to Maghrib, ..."*— Translator.

[56] *"When the Salah has begun (by reciting the Iqamah) and supper is brought then give priority to the supper."* Reported by the Two Sheikhs from Anas and from Ibn 'Umar.'

that a Muslim should not perform the *Salah* while his mind is engaged with other than communion with Allah. After the *Salah*, a Muslim may take the opportunity to discharge some obligations before he goes to bed; for example, visits or courtesy calls.

It behoves a Muslim to have a daily slot of disciplined study in his quest to increase his knowledge, just as Allah instructed His Messenger:

"...And say, 'My Lord! Increase me in knowledge.'"
(Suratu Ta-Ha 20: 114)

It will be a good idea for him if he selects books and journals that will benefit him in his religious and earthly life. A wise man once said, *"Tell me what you read, and I shall tell you who you are!"*

There is no blame upon a Muslim if he entertains himself with permissible pastimes and lawful recreation, during the day or at night, on the condition that this does not infringe upon the right of his Lord in worship, or the right of his body for rest, or the right of care for his family, or the right of his work for excellence, or any of the rights of others.

It is therefore not proper for a Muslim to stay up late at night, as this may cause him to transgress upon some of these rights. This is so, even when it may not directly be his intention to transgress any right, for it is difficult to find an excess in one area that is not accompanied by a loss in another. Furthermore, such excesses are contrary to what the Merciful Lord has commanded, and what the Qur'an teaches.

"That ye transgress not (due) balance, but observe the measure with justice and fall not short in the balance."
(Suratur Rahman 55: 8-9)

Another obligation which a Muslim must daily keep in mind, is never to be lax with regard to any of the Ten Rights which Allah {SWT} has commanded to be observed when He says:

"Serve Allah, and join not any partners with Him; and do good to parents, kinsfolk, orphans, those in need, neighbours who are of kin, neighbours who are strangers, the companion by your side, the wayfarer (ye meet), and what your right hands possess."

(Suratun Nisa 4: 36)

The first of these rights, and the most important, is the right of Allah {SWT}, the Creator of creation, the Owner of the Command, the Donor of Life, and the Bestower of all Comforts:

"And whatever of comfort ye enjoy, it is from Allah...."

(Suratun Nahl 16: 53)

Therefore, it is not permissible for a Muslim to disrespect the rights of Allah, or be unmindful of them.

The most prominent of the daily rights of Allah {SWT} is the *Salah*. Allah has made humility in *Salah* the first distinguishing mark of the Believers: *"Those who humble themselves in their Salah"*[57] and the last distinguishing mark is its strict observance: *"And those who (strictly) guard their Salawat."*[58] Allah {SWT} has ordained eternal misery and perdition for those who are too busy for it until its specified time lapses: *"So woe to the worshippers; who are neglectful of their Salawat."*[59]

The second of these rights is the right of parents. Hence, being good to them comes, in the Book of Allah, immediately after the right of Allah to exclusive and sincere worship.

The Qur'an and the Sunnah (i.e. the practices and precepts of the Noble Prophet) have given special regard for the mother, as her right is more imperative, her need for care greater, and her responsibility for her child more onerous:

---

[57] Suratul Mu'minun (23: 2)

[58] Suratul Muminun (23: 9)

[59] Suratul Ma'un (107: 4-5)

"In pain did his mother bear him, and in pain did she give him birth, and the carrying of the child to his weaning is (a period of) thirty months."

(Suratul Ahqaf 46: 15)

It is not acceptable in Islam for the mother to have a special day set aside in the year called *Mothers' Day*. Islam desires all days to be Mothers' Days.

After the rights of the parents, come the rights of the relatives - brothers, sisters, maternal and paternal uncles and aunts, cousins, and such like.

Then come the rights of the weak ones in society - the orphans, the poor and the wayfarers. There are also the rights of scores of others from among one's near and distant neighbours, and the companions of a journey or of the home, whether they be temporary or permanent in life, such as the wife in relation to the husband, and vice versa.

At the end of this hierarchy of rights, are the rights of those under your control, in the terminology of the Qur'an, *"what your right hands possess"*. Even though this was applied, in the days of slavery, to the slaves and the obligation of doing good to them, it is a sufficiently elastic phraseology which covers everything that is under ones control, ranging from animals, equipment, tools and objects. In respect of all these, the Believer is under divine command to look after them well. He does this by properly taking care of them and maintaining them; he uses them carefully and responsibly but not arbitrarily, for he is a trustee over them who should bequeath them in a good state to posterity.

Finally, when a Muslim intends to lie down to sleep, it is recommended that he make ablution, perform two *raka'ah* of *Salah*, then retire to bed, lying on his right side, and remembering Allah through any of the bedtime memorials transmitted from the Prophet (Peace and Blessings of Allah be upon him). For example, the Prophet's saying:

"In Your name, my Lord, do I lay my side (on the bed), and in Your name do I raise it. If You withhold my soul (in my sleep), then do have mercy upon it.[60] *And if You send it back (to me), then do guard it as You guard therewith Your righteous servants"*[61]

A Muslim should endeavour to benefit from the books authored by our learned men explaining the various devotional utterances and actions required of him in the morning and in the evening, during the day and at night, for example:

1. *Amalul Yawm wal Lailah* by Imam An-Nasa'i

2. The book with the same title, by his student, Hafiz Ibn as- Sunni

3. *Al-Adhkar* by Imam An-Nawawi

4. *Al-Kalimut Tayyib* by Shaikhul Islam Ibn Taymiyyah

5. *Al-Wabilus Sayyib* by his student, Imam Ibn Qayyim

6. *Al-Hisnul Haseen* by Allamah Ibn al-Jazari, and its commentary and substantiation by Imam Ash-Shawkani in *Tuhfatudh Dhakireen*

7. A number of books written by contemporary authors, of which I recommend *Al-Ma'thurat* – an epistle by Imam Hasan al-Banna. I would also here recommend *Hisnul Muslim,* an invaluable pocketsize booklet comprising *adhkar* from the Qur'an and the Sunnah, compiled by Sheikh Sa'eed bin Wahaf Al-Qahtani and rendered into English by Isma'il Ibrahim, under the title *Fortification of the Muslim.* Another excellent translation (including transliteration) has been prepared by Omar Johnstone, under the title *"Citadel of the Muslim".* – Translator.

---

[60] See Qur'an 39: 42. —Translator.

[61] Reported by the Two Sheikhs from Abu Hurairah. —Translator.

Between the Past, Present and Future

The time within which we live is divided into three: the Past, the Present and the Future; or Yesterday, Today and Tomorrow.

People may become so obsessed with a particular category that they fail to consider it in its wholesome entity. Thus there are those who are enslaved by the Past, those who worship the Present, and those who are devoted to the Future.

There are those who are moderate and balanced in their position, who give each of the three subdivisions of Time its due, without exceeding proper bounds and without forfeiting anything, but they are remarkably few in number.

Those Who Cling to the Past

Among the people, there are some who scarcely acknowledge any time but the Past. They live only in the Past and are oblivious of the facts and realities of Today, and unconcerned with the dreams and aspirations for Tomorrow. It does not make any difference whether this Past is a personal past, or a national and racial past.

One who is enslaved by the past, may manifest this condition in a variety of ways:

(a) He may appear in the garb of a person trying to revive a glorious past; one who takes pride in its grandeur but who adds nothing new, nor brings any improvement that would link it with the present. Such a person continually says, *"We were..."*, or *"Our fathers and grandfathers were...."*. He hardly finds anything worthy that could make him proudly say: *"We have achieved such and such"*, or *"We have accomplished this and that"*.

It is to the likes of these, that Al-Mutanabbi says:

"If indeed ye take pride in noble forefathers, ye have
indeed been true;
Wretched, however, is the child that they have
given birth to."

And another (poet) says:

"Be ye the descendant of whom ye may,
And do ye acquire education;
Its encomiums will make you dispense with genealogy;
The hero is he who says: Look, it is Me;
Not a hero is he who says: My father was."

Taking pride in the grandeur of the past and the glorious deeds of forefathers, is indeed a commendable thing, if it induces one to complete what they have started and emulate their good deeds. However, not to go further than glorifying them over this, is a manifestation of negativism which does not in the least help in nation-building.

What does it benefit rotten bones to say, *"We were once part of a living body"?* The positive attitude here is that described by a poet, when he says:

"We, even though our past was a glorious one,
On our forefathers we never seek to depend;
We build even as our forefathers were wont to build,
And assiduously perform in the same fashion they did."

(b)   A picture that is closely akin to the one just painted, is that of the guardians of the heritage, who call for the sanctification of the heritage in its totality, including its blunders and achievements, the trivial and the serious. They assert that the Past is always better than the Present, that the predecessors have left no stone unturned, and that it is not possible to improve upon what they have done.

To be sure, what is necessary here is to properly define the notion of heritage and, thereafter, evaluate it.

The Muslims include the Qur'an and the Sunnah in the notion of heritage. This is something which, by virtue of the contract and requirement of Faith, we must unconditionally preserve:

"It is not fitting for a Believer, man or woman, when a matter has been decided by Allah and His Messenger, to have any option about their affair."
(Suratul Ahzab 33: 36)

Therefore, aspects that relate to the Divine in the heritage, are not subject to choice, nor open to altercation.

However, the *human* aspect of heritage is what needs to be analysed and sifted, in order to distinguish what part of it may be accepted or rejected. In this sphere, there are features that are local rather than universal in character, which accordingly bear the distinctive stamp of their locality, and are, as such, unsuitable for other localities. They also bear features that are historical in nature, i.e. linked to that particular time period, which render them inapplicable in other times[62].

In reaction to the call towards 'Traditionalism' and the preservation of the heritage, there has concurrently been a call towards 'Modernism'.

(c) There is yet another picture of a person who lives in the Past, clinging on to it and following it blindly. It is for the simple reason that this was the way and practice of his forefathers before him. He would not care to test this past, in order to know its Truths and Falsehoods, its

---

[62] For example, the Qur'an says, *'Therefore, make ready whatever is possible for you of strength against them, including **steeds of war**, to strike terror into (the hearts of) the enemies of Allah and your enemies, and others besides...'* (Suratul Anfal 8:60). Yet despite this, it has never been suggested that preparing for war is only possible through maintaining horses, which the Qur'an specifically mentions. Rather, every sensible person who has an appreciation of the language and the law, has understood the steeds of this age to be tanks, artillery and other such weaponry. – Translator.

Rights and Wrongs. His role, therefore, is that of a receiver-transmitter, not of a discerning experimenter; the role of a follower, not of an entrepreneur.

It is in respect of a similar attitude that the Qur'an says:

"When it is said to them, 'Follow what Allah has revealed', they say, 'Nay! We shall follow the ways of our fathers.' What! Even though their fathers were void of wisdom and guidance?"
(Suratul Baqara 2: 170)

It is this kind of reasoning that, in the past, stood as a stumbling block in the face of the Messengers of Allah. Thus, the people of Hud (AS) said to him:

"Come thou to us, that we may worship Allah alone, and give up that which our fathers used to worship?"
(Suratul A'araf 7: 70)

And the people of Thamud said to Salih (AS):

"O Salih! Thou have been of us! —a centre of our hopes hitherto! Do thou (now) forbid us the worship of what our fathers worshipped?"
(Suratu Hud 11: 62)

And when Ibrahim (AS) said to his people:

"What are these images, to which ye are (so assiduously) devoted?" They said: "We found our fathers worshipping them."
(Suratul Anbiya 21: 52-53)

And the people of Shu'aib (AS) said to him:

"O Shu'aib! Does thy Salah command thee that we leave off the worship which our fathers practised?"
(Suratu Hud 11: 87)

Accordingly, the Qur'an affirms this behavioural trait:

"Just in the same way, whenever We sent a Warner before thee (Muhammad) to any people, the wealthy ones among them[63] said: 'We found our fathers following a certain religion and we will certainly follow in their footsteps."

(Suratuz Zukhruf 43: 23)

The Qur'an indeed raises objections to this class of people on this kind of intellectual stagnation, this kind of fixation with the ways of the forefathers and blind imitation of them. The Qur'an challenges this class of people with such assertions as:

"What! Even though their fathers were void of wisdom and guidance?"

(Suratul Baqara 2: 170)

"What! Even though their fathers were void of knowledge and guidance?"

(Suratul Ma'idah 5: 104)

"He said: 'What! Even if I brought you better guidance than that which ye found your fathers following?'"

(Suratuz Zukhruf 43: 24)

(d) And again, there is yet another picture of a person who lives in the Past. It is that of a person who always regrets the Past, forever pained by the fortunes and opportunities that have missed him, continually hypothesising and rehearsing expressions of regret: *"Would that I had responded"*, *"Would that I had not reacted"*, *"If only I had done this and that it would have been such and such,"* or *"If only I had hastened to do that or tarried a while, the outcome would have been different."*

---

[63] In other words, the class which benefits from the status quo. Beware, for they are always the opponents of new ideas and social change. —Translator.

This kind of thinking, or feeling, throws a person into a sea of psychological distress, turns his life into an unwarranted nightmare, and afflicts him with a damaging negativism. It has absolutely no use. It has, for this reason, been said: *"Worrying over the past squanders away the present."*

It is no wonder that the Qur'an and the Sunnah disapprove of this behaviour. Allah {SWT} says:

"O ye who believe! Be not like those who disbelieved and said to their brethren when they travelled in the land or were engaged in fighting: 'If they had been (here) with us they would not have died or been killed.' This that Allah may make it a cause of sighs and regrets in their hearts. It is Allah that gives Life and Death, and Allah sees well all that ye do."

(Suratu Aal 'Imran 3: 156)

And the Noble Messenger said: *"A strong Believer is better and preferable to Allah than a weak Believer, but in each one of them there is some goodness. Strive over what will be useful to you and seek the help of Allah. Do not say, 'If only I had acted thus the outcome would have been such and such.' Rather, you should say, 'Thus is the Predestination of Allah, and what He wills He does.' Indeed (the expression) 'If only' turns on the work of the Shaytan."*[64]

This belief in the Predestination of Allah the Exalted, comes into play here as an active, positive, influencing factor, which removes man from the negativism of *"If only"* and *"Would that"* and such expressions, to the positivism of work and a constructive attitude towards the Future.

It is in this regard that the poets in their wisdom say:

"I wish I knew! But of what use to me is "If only"?
Verily "If only" and "If" and "Would that" are a difficulty,

---

[64] Reported by Muslim from Abu Hurairah.

What (opportunity or fortune) has missed me would never be
restored
By "What a pity" nor by "If only" nor by "If I had",
The Predestinations of the Deity and His Judgment have gone
ahead,
So cool off your heart from (the torment) of "Perhaps" and of
"If only".

Those Who Worship the Future

In contrast to these 'pastists', who transgress all limits in their attachment to the Past, we find others who exceed all limits in their attachment to the Future. They turn their backs on the Past and completely renounce their history, the history and experiences of their people and of humanity. They totally discard all the intellectual, religious and cultural heritage of humanity without caring to distinguish and sift what is True from what is False, what is Permissible from what is Prohibited, and what is Profitable from what is Injurious.

They would snap at you: *"Give us respite from generations that have long since been dead and forgotten! Leave us alone to focus our minds on the present generation of youths who will become the leaders and elders of tomorrow; nay, on the young children who would become the youths of tomorrow; nay, on the foetuses who are about to be born and soon to become the young children of tomorrow!"*

At other times they would retort: *"Can't you see that our eyes have not been created and stationed on the back of our heads to be looking backwards into the Past? Rather, they have been created and located on our faces so that we should be looking forward into the Future! Why is it then, you keep bothering us to turn our attention to the Past when it is precisely this that fetters us and slows us down in our progress towards our desired goal?"*

This is what they say, or some words to that effect. What they say may be true if directed towards those who want to remain forever in the Past, oblivious of the claims of Today and the responsibilities for Tomorrow.

However, these statements cannot be true, if their purpose is that people should forget the Past with all that it entails, repudiate the Heritage with all that it contains, and throw doubt on History with all that it carries of lessons, precepts, and hints which guide understanding and the intellect. How excellently corroborative in this regard, is the Word of Allah {SWT} in His Book, which draws our attention to take advantage of History and its precepts:

"Have they not travelled through the earth, so that their hearts (and minds) may thus learn wisdom and their ears may thus learn to hear? For indeed it is not the eyes that grow blind, but it is the hearts, which are within the bosoms, that grow blind."
(Suratul Hajj 22: 46)

Taking a Pessimistic and Hopeless View of the Future

There are those who tend to reflect on the Morrow with pessimism. This kind of contemplation casts blinkers over the vision and impairs the way one perceives life, people, times and places. The pessimist is therefore always miserable and desperate; he has lost faith in the Future and hope of success. He is convinced that things will continue to deteriorate from bad to worse, and that life is but one long night without daybreak, a night over which the sun will never shine. This, no doubt, is a view which shatters and destroys both the person himself and the society around him.

The life of an individual bereft of the illuminating rays of hope, is extremely narrow indeed. In days of old, the poet said: *"How narrow is life, were it not for the extensive possibilities (provided by) Hope!"*

The life of a community bereft of hope is dreary, inactive and lifeless. For had it not been for Hope, no building would have been erected, no tree would have been planted, and no advancement whatever would have been made in knowledge.

The fact is that Religion, History and Reality all teach us that life without hope has no meaning, that there is no room for hopelessness as long as there is life, that with each difficulty there is ease, that at the end of every Night there is a Daybreak, and that no condition is permanent.

Allah {SWT} says:

"Truly no one despairs of Allah's Soothing Mercy except the disbelieving folk."
(Suratu Yusuf 12: 87)

In another sign Allah, the Exalted, says:

"And who despairs of the mercy of his Lord, but those who are astray."
(Suratu Hijr 15: 56)

A poet says:

"Man may certainly be distressed by many an event,
With Allah there's always an exit, a way out,
Its noose'll get tighter till it becomes a ringlet,
Suddenly it vanishes! I had thought there was no way out."

And another poet says:

"Crisis has come to a head,
She'll definitely clear,
Your night already has heralded,
That a sun'll soon appear."

A symptom of hopelessness and pessimism, is the belief that many people now hold, which is that we are today witnessing the end of Time, that the signs of the Hour are already evident, that virtue is in retreat and evil on the increase, that the lamp of religious practice is increasingly getting dimmer on its way to extinguishment, and that very soon unbelief shall pervade the world. All this being the case, there is not much hope for cure, and not much hope for improvement.

They try to prove this pessimistic view by quoting the various *ahadith* that have been reported in connection with civil strife, the end of Time and the portents of the Hour.

The issue is not as simple and straightforward as these people have superficially conceived. What has been mentioned in religious texts regarding the nearness of the Hour and the appearance of its signs, does not mean that it is literally just around the corner, for nearness and remoteness are both relative terms. No one knows, except Allah, whether the Hour is thousands of years away from us, or perhaps much nearer than we imagine! The Qur'an, in this regard, says no more than this: *"Perhaps the Hour may turn out to be nigh."* [65] *"Perhaps the Hour is nigh,"* [66] inasmuch as it also says, *"It shall not come to you but all of a sudden."* [67]

The dispatching by Allah of our Prophet, peace and blessings of Allah be upon him, is in itself, a sign of the Hour. Thus he says, *"I have been dispatched I and the Hour being like these two..."* and (holding out his hand) he juxtaposed his middle and forefingers."[68]

Refraining from working to revive the Islamic Law (the *Shari'ah*), the Islamic Community and the Islamic State, in the idle expectation of the Day of Resurrection, and on the pretext that we have approached the end of Time, is an attitude most vehemently rejected by this Religion.

---

[65] Suratul Ahzab 33: 63

[66] Suratush Shura 42: 17

[67] Suratul A'araf 7: 187

[68] Reported by the Two Sheikhs.

A Muslim has been commanded to work and carry out the Jihad (in other words do his utmost in the cause of Islam) so long as he is alive; and the Muslims, as a community, have been commanded to do likewise up until when the Gate of Repentance is shut— and that shall be in the final days of life in this world, when the cosmic laws laid down by Allah for this life shall fall into disarray, and in the wake of which the sun shall rise from the west:

"...in the day which certain of the Signs of thy Lord do come, no good will it do to a soul to believe then, if it believed not before nor earned righteousness through its Faith."

(Suratul Ana'am 6: 158)

The command from the Noble Prophet has come down to us, to persist in work directed at worldly objectives (and these are of secondary importance in the view of this Religion) until life breathes its last. This is when he says, *"If the Hour arrives and in the hands of one of you there is a date-palm seedling which he can plant before he is overwhelmed by the Hour, then let him do so."*[69]

If a Muslim has been commanded not to leave off his planting work even when he has heard the signal for the Hour, but to complete it to the extent that he can, even when neither he nor those after him are likely to benefit from it, then how much greater is the command when, between us and the Hour, is a long stretch of time which no one knows the duration of except the Creator of this universe, be He glorified?

Work is desirable in its own right, even if it does not bring immediate reward to the worker. If it does so, then the worker will have enjoyed the best of the two worlds; otherwise, he should be satisfied that he has exerted himself and done his best; that he has done what is necessary, absolved himself before Allah, and established a case against the defaulters, who would then have no excuse before Allah, the Exalted.

---

[69] Reported by Ahmad, Al-Bukhari in *al-Adabul Mufrad*.

The following *ahadith* serve to clarify the stance we should take in relation to pessimistic views of the future:

1. At-Tirmidhi has reported from 'Ali bin Abi Talib (may Allah be pleased with him) who said that the Messenger of Allah (SAAS) says: *'"There will be dissensions after I have departed, (so serious and perplexing) like a segment of pitch-dark night." I said, "What is the way out from them, O Messenger of Allah?" He said, "The Book of Allah: in it there is report of the past, description of the future and solution to your problems."'*

2. *"Hasten to perform good deeds, for there will be dissensions (as overshadowing and perplexing) as a segment of a pitch-dark night; a person will wake up in the morning as a believer and end up in the evening as an infidel, and he will be a believer in one evening and by the next morning an infidel: he shall barter away his Religion for some fleeting worldly benefit."* (Reported by Muslim).

3. Abu Dawud, At-Tirmidhi and Ibn Majah have reported from the *hadith* of Abu Tha'alabah al-Khushni: *'"There shall certainly come after you difficult and trying days. To persevere in those days shall be (as painful) as clasping embers. A (persevering) worker in those days shall receive the reward of fifty others like him." I said, "O Messenger of Allah! The reward of fifty others from his generation?" He said, "The reward of fifty others from among you."'*

In some versions of this *hadith*, we find the rationale for the multiplication of this reward, when the Prophet (Peace and Blessings of Allah be upon him) says: *"You do find assistance and support in doing good deeds, they shall have none."*

4. The Two Sheikhs have reported from Hudhaifah bin al-Yaman who said: *'People used to ask the Messenger of Allah (SAAS) concerning Virtue, and I used to ask him concerning Evil out of fear that it may overtake me. I would say, "O Messenger of Allah! We were once engrossed in Ignorance and Evil. Then Allah brought us this Virtue (of Islam). Will there be after this Virtue some evil?" The Prophet said,*

"Yes". I said, "After that evil will there be some virtue?" He said, "Yes, but it shall be smoky." I said, "What is that smoke in it?" He said, "Some people who practise other than what I practise, and seek to find guidance other than my guidance: they will hit and miss." I said, "Then will there be, after that virtue, some evil?" He said, "Yes; Invitors to the Hellfire. Whoever responds to their invitation to it, they shall throw him therein." I said, "O Messenger of Allah! Will you describe them for us?" He then said, "They are a people from our own race and language."'

These *ahadith* should put you on your guard against evil, arouse your desire for virtue, encourage you to be resolute over the truth and urge you to hold fast onto the Book of Allah. They should encourage you to persevere in your obedience to Allah, in holding onto His Rope, and in holding out against the evil people standing over the gates of the Hellfire. Once you hearken to these evil people, and respond to their call, they will throw you into the Hellfire.

Facing the Future with Dreams and Fancies

In contrast to this negative attitude towards the Future— this attitude of hopelessness and pessimism— is another equally negative attitude: the attitude which approaches the Future with nothing more than fancies and empty dreams, rather than with knowledge, action and planning.

Fancies neither confer respectability, nor realise any hope. They are no more than what Ka'ab bin Zuhair says about them: *"Fancies and dreams are delusions!"*

Someone said to Ibn Sirin: *"In my sleep I see myself swimming, but not in water; and flying without wings! What meaning do you ascribe to this dream?"* He said to him: *"You are a man with many fancies and dreams!"*

And 'Ali bin Abi Talib said to his son: *"Beware of relying on fancies; they are the wares of the imbecile."*

And a poet says:

"My heart often I would entertain with a fancy,
To find rest, perhaps, from overwhelming fancies,
Very well I know you cannot be attained,
Yet my fancy I shall continue to sustain".

And another poet says:

"Yourself allow not to be enslaved to fancies,
For fancies are the capital of those in bankruptcy!"

It is no surprise that the Qur'an rebukes the People of the Book, from the Jews and the Christians, for clinging to fancies over their certainty that they will be admitted into the Garden, even without possessing the means and the requirements of Faith and Good Deeds.

Allah {SWT} says:

"And they say, 'None shall enter Paradise unless he be a Jew or a
Christian.' Those are their (vain) desires. Say, 'Produce your proof
(of what ye state) if ye are truthful.' Nay, whoever submits his whole
self to Allah and is a doer of good, he will get his reward with his
Lord; and on such shall be no fear, nor shall they grieve."
(Suratul Baqara 2: 111 – 112)

The Qur'an does not stop at rebuking the People of the Book. It includes with them those Muslims who believe likewise, who think that the mere carrying of a tag of Islam shall confer salvation upon them from Allah. Allah says:

"It will not be in accordance with your desires, nor the desires of the
People of the Book. Whoever works evil will be requited accordingly,
and will not find, besides Allah, any protector or helper. And if any do
deeds of righteousness— be they male or female— and have faith, they
will enter Paradise, and not the least injustice will be done to them."
(Suratun Nisa 4: 123-124)

The Qur'an rebukes and rejects reliance on Fancies, but not Hope. The distinction between the two is that Hope is a desire accompanied by action, whereas Fancy is no more than a passive dream.

Some people give a free rein to their desires and indulge in every passion. They rely on Allah's Forbearance, His Forgiveness and Ample Mercy, even though He says:

"Verily the mercy of Allah is (always) near to those who do good."
(Suratul A'araf 7: 56)

And He also says:

"And My mercy extends to all things. That (Mercy) I shall ordain for those who do right, and pay Zakah and those who believe in Our Signs."
(Suratul A'araf 7: 156)

For this reason, a *hadith* of the Prophet (SAAS) counts such behaviour as weakness and folly. It says: *"The wise person is the one who disciplines and controls himself, and strives for the life hereafter; whilst the weak person is the one who gives free rein to the desires of his heart and he has all kinds of expectations from Allah."*[70]

As for Hope, the Qur'an speaks highly of it, and praises those who exhibit it. An instance of this is where Allah {SWT} says:

"Verily those who believed and those who suffered exile and fought (and strove and struggled) in the path of Allah, they have the hope of the Mercy of Allah: and Allah is Oft-forgiving, Most Merciful,"
(Suratul Baqara 2: 218)

Some pious men say: *"Wishing for the Paradise without striving for it, is (in itself) a sin too many; wishing for Intercession (of the Prophet)*

---

[70] Reported by At-Tirmidhi, Ahmad and Ibn Majah.

without following his Sunnah, is a variety of delusion; and wishing for the Mercy of Allah whilst disobeying Him, is foolishness and ignorance."

Al-Hasan al-Basri says:*'Behold! Some people were carried away by the desire for Allah's Mercy until they departed the world without a single good work to their credit. One of them would say, "I think well of my Lord!" He was lying; if he had thought well of his Lord he would have worked righteousness for His sake.'* Then (to corroborate his statement) he read out the proclamation of Allah, the Exalted:[71]

"Now you see! This thought of yours which ye did entertain concerning your Lord, has brought you to destruction, and (now) ye have become of those utterly lost!"
(Suratu Fussilat 41: 23)

Al-Hasan al-Basri also used to say: *"O mankind! Beware of these desires, for they are valleys of fools who fall into them. Most certainly, Allah does not grant any blessing, neither in this world nor in the life hereafter, by a mere wish"*.

The Worshippers of the Present Moment

There are some people who neither pay attention to the Past, nor consider the Future. They exist purely in the Present Moment. The Past is gone, what is gone is dead, and what is dead is not fit to be considered or preoccupied with.

The Future has not come yet, so in their opinion it is an unknown entity which a realistic person ought not to rely upon, as to do so would be as transient as building on shifting sand and as futile as writing on water.

---

[71] This is a scene from the Day of Judgment. —Translator

They become so engrossed in their involvement with the Present that this distracts them from peering into their Future, even as it distracts them from benefiting from their Past.

As a result, they care nothing for the life hereafter, since that is in the Future. They would rather a bird in the hand than a firm promise of superior millions in the bush; they would prefer to stick to coin and laugh at long-term credit. They do not involve themselves with history and heritage, as that is all in the past and nothing more. These are the *"children of their times"* who neither consider nor attach importance to anything other than the here and now which they live, experience and enjoy. Why would they spoil their day with the thought of tomorrow or yesterday? *"Live for the present!"* – a popular saying.

Now if man has nothing of Time but the hour or moment he lives in, why then does he squander it away? Why does he not exploit it in obedience to Allah, and in the cause and service of the Truth, in doing that which is righteous, and advocating that which has universally been accepted as good?

Thus, the pious man says:

> *"This life is but a Fleeting Pleasure,*
> *The gullible, ignorant is the one who thus prefers her.*
> *The Past is gone, and arrived not has the Future,*
> *Of Time, the Hour you live in, yes, thou art the possessor."*

In other words, man should seize the moment, because, in truth, the Present is but an imaginary line situated between the Past and the Future. It is this that has prompted a poet to say:

> *"What is Time but two moments: You ponder*
> *Over the Past, and speculate on the Future."*

And 'Abdullah Yusuf 'Ali in his commentary on the Qur'an (Suratu Ya Sin 36: 45) has said:

"Man should consider and beware of the consequences of his past and guard against the consequences of his future. The present is only a fleeting moment poised between the past and the future, and gone even while it is being mentioned or thought about."

The Correct Conception of Time

The correct, Islamic view, is one which brings together and integrates the Past, the Present and the Future.

Reviewing the Past:

It is necessary to study the events of the Past, to learn from the fate of its various nations, and to take heed of the events visited upon them by Allah {SWT} in His Wisdom and Supreme Justice. Allah {SWT} says:

"Systems have passed away before you: travel through the land, and see what was the end of those who rejected the Truth. Here is a plain statement to men, a guidance and instruction to those who fear Allah! So lose not heart, nor fall into despair: for ye must gain mastery if ye are true in Faith. If a wound has touched you, be sure a similar wound has touched the others. Such days (of varying fortunes) we give to men and men by turns."
(Suratu Aal 'Imran 3: 137 - 140)

"How many of the Prophets fought (in Allah's way) and with them (fought) large bands of godly men? But they never lost heart if they met with disasters in Allah's way, nor did they weaken (in will) nor gave in. And Allah loves those who are firm and steadfast."
(Suratu Aal 'Imran 3: 146)

"Do they not travel through the land, so that their hearts (and minds) may thus learn wisdom and their ears may thus learn to hear? Truly it is not the eyes that are blind, but the hearts which are in their breasts.
(Suratu Hajj 22: 46)

Yet another reason for looking into the Past, is in order to benefit from the heritage that has been bequeathed to posterity by its ancestors: the heritage of knowledge, literature and the arts, from which we take what is suitable for our time and circumstances.

It has been reported in the *hadith* that: *"Wisdom is the lost property of a believer, wherever he finds it (he picks it up for) he is its rightful owner."*[72]

It is improper to reject and ignore that which is old on the simple pretext that it is old, as there are things for which old-age is a merit and distinction and which, by their very nature, are not amenable to regeneration. Does not the superiority of the Qur'an lie in the fact that it is the Word of Allah whose newness is ever so fresh, and does not wear out with the passage of Time and the centuries?

Does not the superiority of the Ka'aba arise from the fact that it is the *"Ancient House"* to which pilgrimage has purposely been made annually over successive centuries?[73]

The Qur'an does not transform anew, nor does the Ka'aba, nor do facts and reality.

The advocates of reform overstated their case when they discarded all antiquity and welcomed every reform, despite the fact that there are old things which are most useful and new things which are extremely harmful.

---

[72] Reported by At-Tirmidhi and Ibn Majah. (There is a weakness in its chain of transmitters).

[73] The Noble Qur'an says: *"Then let them complete the rites prescribed for them, perform their vows, and (again) circumambulate **the Ancient House**."* (Suratul Hajj 22: 29) —Translator.

Mustafa Sadiq ar-Rafi'i, the Arab Islamic writer, speaks mockingly of them when he says: *"These people want to modernise (the) religion, (the) language, the sun and the moon!"*

Shawqi, the Prince of Poets, speaks of them in his poem on *"Al-Azhar"*. On that occasion he was exposing his opponents who were making pretensions to reform. He says:

> *"Follow not in the footsteps of a group that has been captivated,*
> *Every old thing they came across they had swiftly rejected,*
> *Ancestors, nay living fathers, in public, if they could, they would*
> *put down,*
> *Zealous and scheming in old things, to quickly pull them down,*
> *Yet incapable when charged, an edifice to put up (not to pull*
> *down)."*

In any case, oldness and newness are relative terms. Many a time, a thing that may be old in the opinion of some people, may be new to others; and many a time, a new thing in a given environment, may be old in another. Moreover, the new does not remain new and ageless forever; that which is old today was new yesterday, and that which is new today shall become old tomorrow.

It is necessary for an individual to pause at the end of each day that has passed, in order to check himself and run through his achievements: What has he done in the course of the day? Why has he done it? What has he omitted? Why has he omitted it?

How excellent it would be if this self-criticism were to take place before one retired to bed.

This period of self-criticism and appraisal should certainly be counted among man's moments of progress; it is a moment when man impartially sits as a judge over himself and reviews his yearnings and inclinations, his instincts and motivations. It is a moment when the believer appoints, out of his conviction, a policeman to watch over himself, an investigator to probe him, and a judge to condemn or acquit him. In this way he progresses from the state of *"the soul that incites to evil"* to the state of *"the self-reproaching soul"* which reproaches its owner whenever he plunges into sin, or falls short of expectation.

In a *hadith* we quoted before it was said: *"It behoves any sane person to have four periods of time"* and one of the four periods is *"a period in which he engages in self-criticism."*

The Commander of the Faithful, 'Umar bin al-Khattab says: *"Criticise and appraise yourselves before you are criticised and appraised (on the Day of Judgement), and weigh out your deeds, before they are weighed out for you."*[74]

'Umar himself, may Allah be pleased with him, used to whip his foot at night and say to himself: *"Tell me, what have you done today?!"*

Maimun bin Mahran, a famous companion of the Prophet, used to say: *"A pious person scrupulously examines and appraises himself more than he would a tyrant ruler and a tight-fisted partner!"*

Al-Hasan said: *"A believer polices his own Self; he criticises and appraises it for the sake of Allah. The Final Appraisal (Hisab) may turn out to be mild on some people simply because they were wont to appraise themselves in this life; and the Final Appraisal on the Day of Resurrection may turn out to be rigorous on a people who took this life with levity, and thought they would not be called to account".*

Then he described how this self-criticism and appraisal operates in practice: *"'A fascinating thought (or idea) suddenly comes to the mind of a believer. He says to himself: "By Allah this is fascinating, I need it! But no, never. Get lost! I am prohibited from executing you!"'*
(This is self-criticism and appraisal *before* the event).

---

[74] The Noble Qur'an says: *"On that Day will men proceed in groups, sorted out, to be shown their Deeds (that they had done). Then shall anyone who has done an atom's weight of good, see it! And anyone who has done an atom's weight of evil, shall see it."* (Suratul Zulzilah 99: 6-8). — Translator.

And: "*A believer may inadvertently do something. He would then turn to himself and say: "What do you mean by this? By Allah, I cannot find an excuse for this. I shall never repeat it, insha'Allah!"*" (This is self-criticism and appraisal *after* the event).

If a Believer fails to observe this brief period of soul-searching daily, then he should at least try to do so once every few days, or once a week. In this way, he draws up his life balance sheet, depicting to him his (spiritual) assets and liabilities.

A Believer should also have a longer period of this practice at the end of each month, and an even longer period at the end of the year, when he bids farewell to one year and prepares for and welcomes another. This is the time to critically review the Past and plan for the Future. This is the (spiritual) equivalent of his final accounts for the year.

One blameworthy innovation initiated by the West and unfortunately imitated by some Muslims, is the annual birthday celebration, where people are invited to a party and served with delicious food and drink.

At times, people obsequiously yield to meaningless rituals and imitative practices for which Allah has sent down no authority. For example, they light a number of candles, each one representing a year in the lifetime of the celebrant. Having lit the candles, the celebrant then histrionically proceeds to blow them out. Gifts are presented and pleasantries exchanged on the occasion.

Rather than this blind, useless imitation, it is better for an intelligent and sensible person to seize this occasion, which marks the expiry of one year of his lifetime, to reconsider and reflect upon his life. At the end of every year, a careful trader applies the brakes in order to measure his performance over the past year, and establish his financial position at the end of it. He wants to know his profit or loss, and his assets and liabilities; i.e. his claims and the claims against him. An intelligent, sensible person ought to do likewise, in respect of his life. More than that, he should beseech Allah to bless his life, make his day better than yesterday, and his tomorrow better than today.

It is worthier for an intelligent and sensible person to call himself to account for one whole year of his life that has expired, in respect of which Allah, the Exalted, will question him. A year is not a short time. It is a period of twelve months; a month is on average thirty days; each day has twenty-four hours, each hour sixty minutes, and each minute sixty seconds. And every second should be counted as a blessing, a favour upon him from Allah and a trust from Allah in his hands.

It is worthier for this intelligent and sensible person to commiserate with himself over the turning of a page in the book of his life. Each day that passes is, as it were, a leaf that has withered and fallen from the tree of his life. May Allah have mercy on Al-Hasan al-Basri when he says: "*O son of Adam! You are but a bundle of days. As each day passes away, a portion of you vanishes away!*"

Abu 'Ali ad-Daqqaq used to chant the following lines:

"Each day that passes, a portion of me it takes away,
On the heart, a bitter taste it leaves, and then glides away."

Another poet says:

"Man rejoices as long as the nights continue to pass by,
Yet, he too, as they vanish gradually perishes away."

Yet another poet says:

"We take delight in every day that we have lived,
Yet each day that passes is a portion (gone) of a lifetime."

This is the view that every intelligent and sensible person ought to take. However, intelligent and sensible people are few in this world.

Considering the Future:

Man, by his very nature and constitution, is inextricably bound with the Future. He cannot afford to ignore or be oblivious of it. Just as man is endowed with memory which binds him with the Past and its events, so too he is endowed with imagination, which conjures up the Future for him and its likely occurrences.

One of the characteristics of the Future is that it is hidden and unknown. No one knows what secrets it holds, and what it conceals of good or evil:

No soul knows what it is that it will earn on the morrow."
(Suratu Luqman 31: 34)

Another characteristic of the Future is that whatever it may hold is close at hand, no matter how much man thinks it is distant or slow to arrive. For this reason it is said: *"The Future is already here with the Present; and the Future is ever close to whoever anticipates her."*

Allah, {SWT}, says in the Qur'an:

"And the matter of the Hour (of Judgement) is but as the twinkling of the eye, or even quicker."
(Suratun Nahl 16: 77)

The intelligent, sensible person is one who prepares for the Future and gets ready for an event before it occurs. Allah, {SWT}, says: *"O ye who believe! Observe your duty to Allah. And let every soul look to what (provision) it has sent forth for the morrow"*
(Suratul Hashr 59: 18)

Those who think that this Religion keeps man attached and riveted to the Past, lack the understanding of the essence of this Religion and its reality.

The most eminent function of this Religion is to prepare man for eternal life, that is to say, to prepare him for the Future, for an abode that is better and more lasting.

Hence considering the Future is basic to the foundation of this Religion.

It has been reported in the *hadith* that: *"Man is poised between two apprehensions: a portion of his life that has expired— he does not know what Allah will do concerning it; and a portion of his life that remains — he does not know what Allah has decreed in it. Let man, therefore, make provision for himself from himself, from this Life for the Hereafter, and from youth before old-age. By Him in Whose Hand is my life, no one shall be allowed to make amends after death, and there is no abode after this life except the Garden or Hell".*

To be sure, this *hadith* does not mean that a religious man cares only for his eternal, spiritual future, or that he is oblivious of his earthly future. In truth, Islam has taught the Muslim to care for his Future, to prepare for it, take precautions and employ all means that will assist him achieve his goals, be they in religious or earthly affairs.

When we consider the life of the Messenger of Allah (SAAS), who remains the Perfect Model for the believers, we find him constantly exploring and planning for the future of his Mission. There was the occasion when he took a pledge of allegiance from the tribes of al-Aws and al-Khazraj, and contemplated making the Hijrah, all in the pursuit of a relentless principle: to establish the *Shari'ah* and the Islamic State.

Were not the First and Second Pledges of 'Aqabah, followed by the preparations for the Hijrah to Yathrib (Madina) anything but sustained efforts and well laid out plans for the future of Islam?

And in secular matters, we find the Messenger of Allah (SAAS) stocking one year's provisions for his family. Not for one moment did he consider his action as being contrary to the precept of *Tawakkul* (reliance on Allah), for there is no incompatibility between relying on Allah and making one's own efforts to achieve an end.[75]

---

[75] The Two Sheikhs have reported from 'Umar bin al-Khattab that: *'The property of Banu an-Nadir was part of what Allah caused to revert to the ownership of His Messenger... He used it to provide for his family's needs for a whole year.'* In another text: *'He used it to stock up one year's provision for his family, and the surplus (income) he invested in weapons and steeds in preparation for war in the cause of Allah.'* – Translator.

76

Concern for the Present:

As much as it is necessary for the Believer to sift through the Past for what lessons may be reaped and to consider the Future in order to prepare for it, it is equally necessary for him to focus his attention on the Present, the hour that he resides in and experiences, so that he can exploit it before it slips away.

Imam Abu Hamid al-Ghazali says in his *Ihya' 'Ulum ud-Deen:*

"Hours are of three types: There is the (past) hour which no longer requires any exertion on the part of man, howsoever it was spent, be it luxuriously or in hardship; there is the hour that lies ahead in the future; it has not arrived yet. Man does not know whether he can survive long enough to dwell in it, nor what Allah has decreed in it; there is the present hour, in respect of which he ought to exert himself to the limit and keep his duty to his Lord, so that if the second of the three hours does not meet him (alive) he will have had no cause to regret over it. If it does, he would, while it lasts, equally discharge his responsibility as he had done in the previous hour."

"Let him entertain a life expectancy of less than fifty years. An expectation beyond that may cause monotony and break his resolve to all along exert himself and keep his duty to his Lord. No; he should be temporal: 'a child of the hour', who thus exploits his present moments as if— who knows?— they were his last. Now suppose these were indeed his last moments. It thus behoves him to (always) be in such a condition as he would not abhor death to take him in. His condition shall be confined to what Abu Dharr, may Allah Ta'ala be pleased with him, reported from the Prophet (SAAS): 'A Believer does not become motivated except on three occasions: making provision for the Hereafter, seeking livelihood, or pursuing a pleasure which is not prohibited.'"

"*His position shall be defined and circumscribed by what was, in the same vein, again reported by Abu Dharr from the Prophet: 'It behoves an intelligent man to have four time periods: a period which he communes with his Lord; a period in which he cross-examines himself; a period in which he reflects over the (wonders of) creation of Allah, the Exalted; a period which he devotes to his needs for food and drinks'. This (fourth) period reinforces him in the other three. Even then, this period— in which he exerts himself for his livelihood— should not be devoid of the most important work: that is contemplation and the remembrance of Allah. For even in the food that he eats, for example, there are some wondrous things which, if only he would contemplate and comprehend them, would have been more rewarding than many of his manual deeds.*"

A poet says:

> "*Your day, Yesterday, passed away being a just witness,*
> *To Today you've arrived against you she too is a witness,*
> *In the course of Yesterday if you perpetrated some weakness,*
> *For praise then, follow it up Today with a goodness,*
> *Delay not for a day to Tomorrow an act of goodness,*
> *Tomorrow, maybe, arrives and you're gone: you're not death-*
> *less,*
> *Your day, if you delight her, to you returns her goodness,*
> *A flowing river— she does not, and never shall retrogress.*"

One of the most admirable things ever said in motivating people to work for a living and to discharge the responsibilities of the present moment, is this wonderful *hadith* of the Prophet (SAAS), which we have quoted previously. In it, the Prophet (peace and blessings of Allah be upon him) says: "*If the Hour arrives and in the hands of one of you there is a date-palm seedling which he can plant before he is overwhelmed by the Hour, then let him do so.*"

We should pause here for an analytical review of this extremely amazing *hadith* and ask why the Messenger of Allah (SAAS) instructs the holder of the date-palm seedling, (on the verge of the Hour), to plant it if he is able? This man is not going to survive long enough to reap the fruits of his labour. Neither is he, under these circumstances, planting today so that he could harvest tomorrow.

His case is not that of a person who plants what he plants for posterity, like the case of an extremely old man who was planting an olive tree and was asked (in amazement): *"Why are you planting this when you are on the brink of death?"* He (wittily) replied: *"Those before us planted so that we should eat thereof; we plant so that those after us can eat."*

However, under the circumstances mentioned by the *hadith*, no one is going to survive to eat from what has been planted today, since the Hour is upon them.

It is clear that this instruction is meant to accord dignity to labour in its own right, whether or not someone is likely to benefit from its fruit. It is a declaration to the effect that a Muslim person never ceases to cultivate the land and produce for life, and he does not refrain from work so long as life persists. It is not permissible for him to live for one moment without working, even if the angel Israfil has already seized the Trumpet and is about to blow it (to herald the Hour), from which time all the structures of life will tumble down.

The planting of a date-palm seedling in circumstances like these, denotes the importance of discharging the rights and obligations of the Present Moment, the independent rights and obligations of the here and now without reference to the Future or the Past.

Prolonging Life through Good Deeds

It is an incontestable fact that man, quite naturally, loves life and desires to live long, or forever if it were possible. It was through this natural instinct, this innate desire for eternal life, that Iblis, the Wretched One, was able to reach out to Adam, the Father of Mankind, and deceive him into eating from the Forbidden Tree:

"But the Shaytan whispered evil to him, saying: 'O Adam! Shall I lead thee to the Tree of Eternity and to a kingdom that never decays?"
(Suratu Ta Ha 20: 120)

Furthermore, Islam itself considers long life as a blessing, provided it has been spent in righteousness and the defence of the truth. The Prophet (peace and blessings of Allah be upon him), was asked: *"Who is the best of mankind?"* He said, *"The one whose life is long and deeds are best."*[76]

What is equally incontestable, however, is that death does spoil the pleasure of life. Many a youth has been snatched away by death in the prime of life, a bride on her honeymoon, a lone pampered child from its parents, a comfortable wealthy man from the arms of his comfort and affluence, and a dreaded ruler from under the very eyes of his bodyguards and servants. For this reason, death has been described as: *"The Destroyer of Pleasures, the Separator of Peoples"*.

Now if death is the journey's end, the final terminus of life, then life is but one short struggle, no matter how far one gets carried away by ambition, and how long he has been permitted to live. Life is but a few countable days and breaths which death terminates without notice, casting the deceased into the linguistic dungeon of *"once upon a time"*:

> *"The fate of death is sealed on humanity,*
> *The world is never a permanent abode,*
> *A man may now be basking in the sun of publicity,*
> *A celebrity, but soon he becomes a mere report."*

It has been mentioned in a celebrated *hadith*: *"Live for as long as you may, you are a mortal; love whomsoever you may, you shall separate from them; and do whatever you will, you shall be repaid in the same coin and questioned over it."*[77]

---

[76] Reported by At-Tirmidhi, At-Tabarani, Al-Hakim and Al-Baihaqi.

[77] Reported by At-Tabarani and Ash-Shirazi.

80

Abul 'Atahiyah was right when he said:

"Within my view all living creatures recline,
The tokens of death from them shine,
You should begin to mourn over thine
Own life, you pauper!, if you could,
Thou shall die even if you lived
As long as Prophet Noah did."

Neither medicine, which can now perform heart transplants, nor science, which has launched man on the moon, can forestall senility or transform a grand old man into a youth. The Messenger of Allah (SAAS) was right when he said: *"Allah has not sent down a disease except He had sent down a cure for it, except senility."*[78]

Now if such is the lifetime of man, so inexorably characterised and limited by old-age and death, of what benefit is it then for him to prolong it, and how does he proceed to do so?

The truth is that the real lifetime of man is not the number of years he has spent from the date of birth to the date of death. Rather, his real lifetime is exclusively measured in the number of "time-credits" that have been recorded for him with Allah, as a result of his good works and righteous deeds.

It is not surprising to find an individual who has biologically lived more than one hundred years, yet his stock of time-credits arising from his keeping his duty to Allah, and benefiting his fellow human beings is zero, or less than zero. That is to say, if we should speak the language of bankers, he is in debit.

---

[78] Reported by Al-Bukhari.

By contrast, another person may die in his youth, but his stock of time-credits, garnered over his short life after the age of maturity, is made up of splendid deeds.

The author of Al-Hikam says: *"Many a lifetime may be long but short of resources; and many a lifetime may be short but replete with resources. Whoever is blessed in his lifetime, accomplishes within a short time, by the grace of Allah, feats which are beyond words and imitation."*

It follows, therefore, that one can prolong one's life by worshipping Allah and serving humanity. Each time one's work evinces sincerity and thoroughness, one's merit and reward with Allah become greater.

The value of an individual and his status, is determined by the extent of the effect of his work on the lives of others. He may, for example, lead them to guidance, deliver them from ruin, relieve them of distress, liberate them from tyranny, repel from them an enemy, or other such praiseworthy deeds. These are deeds which benefit the doer as well as other individuals, groups or even the whole of society itself. [79]

For this reason, work such as inviting others to Allah and Jihad in His cause, can easily be considered the highest of all works in prestige with Allah {SWT}. The Messenger of Allah, peace and blessings of Allah be upon him, says: *"Whoever invites (others) to guidance shall have a reward equal to the rewards of those who have followed him (in that guidance): his reward is not a commission paid out to him from their rewards."*[80]

---

[79] The effect and reward of a pious deed like fasting is limited to the one fasting. However, a deed such as imparting knowledge to others, sets up a chain reaction of reward and influence. Which of the two is more useful and rewarding? Imam Ibn Qayyim (RA) concludes that this depends upon the circumstances. The best deed, therefore, is the "deed of the hour", the deed dictated by the logic and requirements of the moment. —Translator.

[80] Reported by Muslim from Abu Hurairah.

Again he says: *"There are one hundred ranks in Paradise. Allah has prepared them for those (mujahidin) who strive their utmost in His cause. The (distance in) distinction between any two ranks is like the (distance) between the heavens and the earth."*[81]

The uprightness and just dispositions of leaders and those entrusted with public offices and positions of authority are worthy of great reward and distinction. This is because of the enormity of the social responsibility placed upon them, and their capacity to bring about the general welfare of large groups of people. It is also due to the heavy demands that these positions of authority make on their holders to strive hard against themselves and to resist their personal inclinations towards favouritism or injustice. On account of all these, it is reported in a *hadith*: *"A day from (the lifetime of) a just leader is better than the worship of sixty years."*[82]

A man from among the Companions of the Prophet (SAAS) passed by a valley containing a spring of fresh, soft water. It captivated him, and he said (to himself): *"How nice it would be if I were to cut off from people and seclude myself in this valley (for worship). I would not do that, however, until I have sought the permission of the Messenger of Allah (SAAS)."* The Prophet said to him: *"Do not do that, for the rank of one of you (for striving) in the cause of Allah, is better than observing the Salah in his house for seventy years. Don't you people like Allah to forgive you and admit you into Paradise? Go on a military expedition in the cause of Allah. Whoever fights in the cause of Allah for a few seconds[83] is entitled to Paradise."*[84]

---

[81] Reported by Al-Bukhari from Abu Hurairah.

[82] Reported by At-Tabarani from *hadith* of Ibn 'Abbas.

[83] What I have here translated as "a few seconds" is *fawaqa naqatin* which, in the process of milking a she-camel, refers to the time interval between two successive squeezes on the udder. —Translator.

[84] Reported by At-Tirmidhi and by Al-Hakim who perfects it on the criterion of Muslim from the *hadith* of Abu Hurairah.

In this manner, deeds excel one another. The eternally fortunate person, therefore, is the one who aspires for the best, as Allah Ta'ala says:

"So announce the Good News (O Muhammad) to My Servants, those who listen to the Word and follow the best of it."
(Suratuz Zumar 39: 17-18)

Many people have had the good fortune of accomplishing glorious deeds in so short a time that their accomplishments have been regarded as little short of miracles. Yet they were not miracles. They were only a blessing and success granted by Allah.

It suffices us to mention here that the Messenger of Allah (peace and blessings of Allah be upon him), delivered mankind from the depths of darkness (of ignorance) to the light (of Islam). He completely altered forever the course and content of human history, all within a span of just twenty-three years. He established a new religion and brought up, on its precepts, a unique generation, organised an exemplary community, and founded a worldwide empire — all within this short period of time, and despite all the difficulties and obstacles that greeted his way right from the outset.

Do not think that the Messenger of Allah (SAAS) was being assisted by miracles, and therefore we cannot emulate his example. For the reality was that the life of the Messenger of Allah (SAAS) in his call and jihad, proceeded in accordance with the familiar laws of Allah. His challenging miracle did not lie in summoning any supernatural phenomena, but in the Noble Qur'an itself.[85] Miracles did come into play, but exclusively in specific circumstances, when everything possible on earth had been done, and nothing else remained but intervention and succour from the heavens. For example, Allah assisted him during the Hijrah (migration from Makkah to Madina), by sending

---

[85] In proof of its authorship coming from Allah, and not a human being, the Noble Qur'an, in many *ayat*, issues a challenge to the whole of mankind to produce, if they are able, a book that could compare to it. It is in the Noble Qur'an that the challenging and permanent miracle of the Prophet (SAAS) lies. —Translator.

down His peace upon him and strengthening him with invisible forces. Likewise during the Battle of Badr, after the Prophet (SAAS) had taken all the necessary steps, Allah assisted him with one thousand angels. In the words of the Noble Qur'an:

> *"Allah made it but a message of hope, and an assurance to your hearts."*
>
> (Suratul Anfal 8: 10)

And consider the feats of the Rightly Guided Caliphs, and of those in their company from among the Companions of the Messenger of Allah (SAAS), and of those who followed them in all good works. See how they made conquests, spread Islam, educated nations and delivered them from their pagan religions and ignorant practices, all within a few score years, to the extent that historians stood bewildered in the face of this revolution in religion, mentality, thoughts, society and politics, brought about in the world by Islam in less than a century!

And consider an individual, like 'Umar bin 'Abdul 'Aziz, who firmly resolved to give back the Caliphate its integrity of conduct, restore trampled rights and stolen property to their owners and *"render back trusts to those entitled to them"*. He set out and went about his mission in the cause of Allah, undeterred and unshaken by criticism.

The weight of a deed increases in the Balance of Truth, and its value and reward increase every time the obstacles on its way multiply, discouragement escalates and helpers are few or non-existent.

It is for this reason that the Companions of the Prophet (may Allah be pleased with them), continue to remain superior in merit to those who came after them. For they believed at a time when others remained unbelievers and they accepted the Faith when other people were rejecting it. The superiority of the first of those who forsook their houses (the Muhajirun) and those who gave them aid (the Ansar) over those who accepted the Faith and joined the Cause later after the Victory[86] is declared in the Noble Qur'an:

"Not equal among you are those who spent (freely) and fought, before the Victory, (with those who did so later). Those are higher in rank than those who spent (freely) and fought afterwards. But to all has Allah promised a goodly reward."
(Suratul Hadid 57: 10)

It is for this reason also, that a good deed has a greater reward and a higher value with Allah, at a time when societies become corrupt and their affairs confused; when the rulers tyrannise, the rich live in opulence, the mighty oppress, the scholars fawn, immorality spreads, evil struts about, and virtue runs for cover. This is a state of affairs which our ancient scholars termed *"the advent of civil strife and corruption of the times"*. We call it *"The Modern-Day Jahiliyyah"*.[87] Those who live by the Religion of Allah, and for the Religion of Allah, in days like these, are akin to a modern-day generation of the Companions, due to the fact that the Religion is beating a retreat, and the Days of Ignorance are on the march again.

It has been reported in a sound *hadith* that the Prophet (SAAS) said: *"Worship in times of turmoil and confusion is (in merit and reward) like migrating to me (from Makkah to Madina).*[88]

Commenting on this *hadith*, Al-Hafiz Al-Mundhari says: *"Turmoil and confusion means civil strife and dissension. In some other ahadith this*

---

[86] The Victory refers to the victory of Islam over the City of Makkah which was, at that time, what London, Washington and Paris are today: centres of evil and conspiracy against Islam. —Translator.

[87] The "Ancient Jahiliyyah" ended with the advent of the civilising and enlightening mission of Islam. See Noble Qur'an 33: 33 and 14: 1. —Translator.

[88] Reported by Muslim, At-Tirmidhi and Ibn Majah from the *hadith* of Mu'aqqal bin Yassar.

has been interpreted as war because strife and dissension are a cause of war. Thus the effect has been substituted for the cause."[89]

Abu Umayyah ash-Sha'abani says: *'I came to Abu Tha'alabah al-Khushni and said to him, "What is your understanding of this sign?" He said, "Which sign is it?" I said: "O ye who believe! Guard your own souls: if ye follow (right) guidance no hurt can come to you from those who stray."[90] He said, "You have asked the right person. I asked the Messenger of Allah* (SAAS) *with regards to it and he said: "Nay, you should enjoin the good and forbid the wrong until you observe that people are motivated by avarice, pursue vain desires, prefer this life, admire their own opinion (only); until you see a situation over which you have no power: then take charge of your own soul. There indeed lie ahead of you days of perseverance: perseverance in them is like clasping embers. Whoever works good deeds in those days shall have a reward equivalent to the reward of fifty others like him."'*

This is a *hadith* reported by Ibn Majah in those words. At-Tirmidhi has also reported it, and says it is a good rare *hadith*; so has Abu Dawud, who reported further: *'It was said: "O Messenger of Allah! Is he going to have the reward of fifty others from among his contemporaries, or from among our generation?" He said, "No, the reward of fifty others from among you."'*

In some reports the Prophet (SAAS) mentions the reason for this fifty-fold increase in reward. He says: *"You have helpers in good causes; they shall have none."* What can be inferred from this *hadith* is that it must have been addressed at a time when Islam had spread, found helpers, and people were embracing it in large numbers, because the first of those who forsook their houses (the Muhajirun), and those who gave them aid (the Ansar), found no helpers at all. Rather, they found a world that was too ready to engage them in war. The whole Arab world

---

[89] *At-Targheeb wat-Tarheeb*, Volume 5, *hadith* number 4,555.

[90] Suratul Ma'idah (5: 105)

was in one camp against them. No one, therefore, approaches their merit and superiority.

The *hadith* makes it imperative to persist in enjoining what is good and forbidding what is wrong, so long as there is an ear that will listen, and a heart that may take heed; and so long as there is hope that someone may, somehow, respond to the Call. However, when all doors are shut in the face of a worker for Islam, all means are severed, and the affair is beyond his capability, as has been mentioned in the *hadith*: "*...and you see a situation over which you have no power...*", then in such a situation the Believer has but one option: to persevere until Allah decrees a matter that He had already decided.

'Perseverance' here does not mean passiveness. It means pausing and waiting for an auspicious moment, with an active heart boiling with rage over the unfortunate state of affairs. That is why the *hadith* compares it to "*clasping embers*".

Perseverance, in the *hadith*, could also mean thinking over, along with other true believers, a profound long-term strategy to fundamentally change the corrupt situation. It is important to work alongside others, as this easily accomplishes what may be impossible for an individual. An individual alone is a minority, but united with his brethren, he becomes the majority. Furthermore, the assistance of Allah is together with the rightful multitude.[91]

Perhaps this is what is meant by the good deed in respect of which its doer is recompensed with the reward of fifty others from among the Companions of the Prophet. This also suggests that the deed itself is of the type accomplished by the Companions: of holding fast to the truth, getting together in support of Islam, challenging the forces of

---

[91] The rightful multitude is ever guided by the light and beauty of the truth and never succumbs to pressure to conform to erroneous beliefs and practices, no matter how popular. See Chapter Ten of Imam Ibn Qayyim's most valuable book *Ighathatul Lahfan* where he discusses the "Symptoms of Diseased and Healthy Minds". — Translator.

Ignorance, sacrificing all in the Cause of Allah, and persevering and encouraging others to persevere, until Allah completes His Light, even though the Unbelievers may detest it.

The Second Lifetime for Man

Similarly, the man who has had the good fortune of managing his time and spending it wisely, can prolong his lifetime and extend it beyond his death, as far as Allah may permit him, so that he continues to live after his death and plays a role in the lives of the living, while he rests in his grave.[92]

This is only possible if he has left behind him a legacy from which mankind continues to derive benefit, even after his death. It may be a legacy of useful knowledge, good deeds, worthy footprints on the sands of history, a precedent that continues to be emulated, a charitable establishment that continues to bring forth its fruits, or well-trained children. All these are extensions of his life and a good commentary on his biography.

In connection with this, Imam Muslim reported in a *hadith* of Abu Hurairah from the Prophet (SAAS): *"When a son of Adam dies, his work ceases except on three accounts: a perpetual charity, a useful knowledge, or a pious child who prays for him."*

In another *hadith*, which elaborates upon these three (facets), it is said: *"Of the works and good deeds of a Believer that catch up with him after his death are: knowledge that he taught and propagated, a pious child he has bequeathed (to society), a literary work that survives him, a mosque he has built, a hospice he has built for travellers, a canal he has constructed, or a charitable endowment which he has settled out of his wealth when he is alive and healthy: all these catch up with him*

---

[92] Extension of lifetimes has been mentioned in sound *ahadith*. For example, *"Whoever it pleases to have his means of livelihood enlarged, and his lifetime extended, then let him take care of his relatives."* Reported by the Two Sheikhs from Anas bin Malik. —Translator.

after his death." (Reported by Ibn Majah with a good chain of transmitters, and also by Al-Baihaqi).

Muslim also reported this in his collection of sound *ahadith*: "*Whoever establishes a good precedent, will have its reward and the reward of everyone who practises it (thereafter) to the Day of Resurrection.*"

And in the Noble Qur'an Allah {SWT} says:

"*Verily We shall give life to the dead, and We record that which they send before and their footprints (which they leave behind)...*"
(Suratu Ya Sin 36: 12)

"*That Day will Man be told (all) that he put forward, and (all) that he put back.*"
(Suratul Qiyama 75: 13)

An honourable mention of a person after his death, is a second lifetime to him – an unlimited lifetime after his limited lifetime. Al-Mutanabbi says:

"*The honourable mention of a man is his second lifetime; his requirement*

Is just what he consumes, all superfluous living is a derangement."

Shawqi adapts this theme with the following vivid verses, in his elegiac poetry on the death of Mustafa Kamil. He says:

"*Man's heartbeats keep on saying to him,*
Life's but minutes and seconds of time,
So raise aloft, for thy Self, her posthumous mention,
For a second lifetime, for man, is good reputation."

It is not surprising, therefore, that in the supplication of the Father of Prophets, the Beloved of the Merciful, Ibrahim (peace be upon him), we find:

> *"And grant me honourable mention on the tongue of truth among later generations."*
>
> (Suratush Shu'ara 26: 84)

There is a world of difference between a man whose death causes hearts to become heavy and grief-stricken, eyes to overflow with tears for him and all tongues to waggle in praise and prayers for him, and a man whose death leaves no eye crying for him, no heart grieving over his departure, and no tongue praying for the repose of his soul, as is the case with one who lived a life of passivity, or an overbearing tyrant. Thus in the latter case a poet says:

> *"That's the one who, if he lives, no one benefits from him,*
> *And if he dies, none of his relatives grieves over him!"*

His case resembles the case of those in respect of whom Allah says:

> *"How many were the gardens and springs they left behind, and cornfields and noble buildings, and pleasant things wherein they had taken such delight! Thus (was their end)! And We made other people inherit (those things)! And neither heaven nor earth shed a tear over them: nor were they given a respite (again)."*
>
> (Suratud Dukhan 44: 25-29)

Many of these wretched specimens of mankind have died but their tyrannies and bestialities, their unbelief and error have refused to die with them. They have already taught and bequeathed them to their pupils and followers, who now most faithfully follow in their footsteps.

Now, if the rule is that whoever establishes a good precedent shall have its reward and the reward of everyone who practises it thereafter to the Day of Resurrection, then whoever establishes an evil precedent, shall bear its burden, and the burdens of everyone who practises it thereafter to the Day of Resurrection.[93]

If the principle is that whoever leaves behind him a legacy of useful knowledge his good work never ceases, then, conversely, whoever leaves behind him a legacy of evil influence and misleading notions and theories, his evil work, likewise, never ceases.

Nothing can be more miserable and burdensome than the punishment of those who have long been dead and buried, yet their bestial deeds, their worthless utterances and their erroneous and misleading thoughts, which have been documented in books and articles, or recorded in films and acted in drama, or captured on cassettes and tape recorders, still circulate and spread like bush fires, corrupting the minds of the people.

This is what has prompted pious people to say: *"Blessed is the person who, when he dies, his evils die along with him, and wretched is the person who, when he dies, his evils persist long after him!"*

Being Wary of Diseases that Kill Time

There are many diseases which dissipate a man's time, and devour his lifetime if he fails to wake up to their seriousness. Some of these diseases are:

Heedlessness:

---

[93] *"Whoever invites (others) to guidance"*, says the Prophet (SAAS), *" shall have a reward equal to the rewards of those who followed him (in that guidance): his reward is not a commission paid out to him from their rewards. And whoever invites (others) to error, shall bear a burden equal to the burdens of those who followed in his footsteps: that will not reduce anything from their burdens."* Reported by Muslim, Ahmad and four others from Abu Hurairah. —Translator.

This is a disease which affects the heart and the intellect of man, such that he becomes unconscious, insensitive and indifferent to events and to the daily changes that take place around him. He loses the ability to read between the lines, interpret events and foresee their consequences. He takes interest in the form rather than the substance, external appearances rather than essential realities, the shell rather than the kernel, and the beginnings rather than the ends of affairs.

The Noble Qur'an cautions very strongly against heedlessness, to the extent that it consigns the heedless to Hell and puts them down as being worse than dumb animals. Thus it says:

"Many are the Jinns and men We have made for Hell: they have hearts wherewith they understand not, eyes wherewith they see not, and ears wherewith they hear not. They are like cattle— nay, they are more misguided: for they are heedless".
(Suratul A'araf 7: 179)

It also condemns those who are mainly concerned with the external and superficial aspects of knowledge, rather than its profound content and intrinsic value. In this regard, it says:

"But most of mankind know not. They know but the outer (things) in the life of this world: but of the Hereafter they are heedless."
(Suratur Rûm 30: 6-7)

It addresses the Messenger of Allah (SAAS) saying:

"And do thou (O Muhammad) remember thy Lord in thy (very) soul, with humility and awe, and without raising your voice, in the mornings and evenings; and be not thou of those who are heedless."
(Suratul A'araf 7: 205)

And in another *ayah*, it says:

"And obey not him whose heart We have made heedless of Our remembrance, who follows his own desires, and his affair has become all excess."

(Suratul Kahf 18: 28)

It is a calamity indeed that momentous events, such as would move the mountains, take place in and around our society yet they are passed over, and they do not alter the society nor shake it out of its slumber. They come to pass as if they were merely a drama or a play being performed.

For this reason, Abu Bakr (may Allah be pleased with him) used to say in his supplication:

"O Allah! Do not forsake us in hardship, do not catch us unawares, and do not put us down among the heedless."

And Sahl bin 'Abdullah used to say: *"Beware of the company of three types of men: scholars who flatter, ignorant mystics and heedless tyrants!"*

Procrastination:

There is yet another disease which is most dangerous to man's enjoyment of his day and his present moments. It is procrastination and postponement. It could become a distinctive habit and a characteristic feature of his personality.

A man from 'Abdul Qais was asked for advice. He said, *"Beware of procrastination."*

Another man says, *"Procrastination is a soldier in the troops of the Shaytan!"*

Your day has a right over you, that you populate and fill it up with useful knowledge and good deeds while it lasts, and before it lapses into a yesterday which never returns. It is a right not to defer its due share to tomorrow. You have a duty, therefore, to cultivate and plant your day, so that you can harvest on the morrow. Otherwise you will regret when regret shall be of no use. In the words of a poet:

> *"On the Day of Resurrection nothing thou shall have except,*
> *That which, before death, you sent forth for the Harvest,*
> *If you did not sow and you subsequently see nothing to harvest,*
> *Your neglect during the planting season thou shalt now regret."*

Imam al-Hasan al-Basri says: *"Beware of procrastination. You fulfil and actualise yourself through Today not Tomorrow. If Tomorrow is granted to you, you will spend it in the manner you will have (seriously) spent Today. If not, you shall have no cause to regret having spent Today the way you did."*

Muhammad bin Samurah, the Traveller, wrote this letter to Yousuf bin Asbaat: *"Dear Brother, Beware not to give authority to Procrastination over yourself, nor give it a foothold in your heart. It is a hideout for fatigue, a refuge for ruination. In it hopes are killed, and with it deadlines are frustrated. If you give chance to Procrastination you will, in effect, have betrayed it into your desire and determination. Reclaim for yourself the zeal that boredom may have seized from you. For unless you do so, you shall not benefit anything from (the use of) your body. Hurry up, my brother! Remember you will be taken unawares. Be quick! For you are on the express lane (to death). Be firm, for it is a serious affair. Arise from your slumber, and be vigilant! Remember your past, your shortcomings, your excesses, your Deeds and Misdeeds. All these have been (immutably) preserved and shall be called to account. It looks as if you have been lax with the affair: so take delight in what you have achieved, and regret over what you have neglected."*

Risks Associated with Procrastination

We have identified four particularly dangerous risks associated with procrastination and the postponement of today's duties and responsibilities to tomorrow:

1) No one is sure whether or not they will live until tomorrow, so to put something off until tomorrow may mean not doing it at all, and thereby losing its rewards.

An emir invited a devout man to a meal. The man declined the invitation and excused himself, saying he was fasting. The emir said to him: *"Break your fast today and fast tomorrow."* The man replied: *"Will you guarantee me that I shall live to tomorrow?"*

There is not a person in the world who can guarantee someone that they will survive to the following day! Death comes unexpectedly and in many ways. A devout poet says:

> *"Make a provision of piety for you know not (the day),*
> *When the night falls if you'll survive the next day,*
> *For many a healthy person has died without a malady,*
> *And many a diseased person has lived many a long day,*
> *Many are the youths who survive, confidently, to a day,*
> *Unknown to them that their shrouds've already been sewn*
> *that day."*

Sudden death, in our day, is more frequent than in the past, despite advances in science and medicine. Medicine cannot stop death by road accidents, assassinations, etc. and science cannot prevent deaths caused by innumerable daily accidents arising from operating modern mechanical and electrical machines such as cars and aeroplanes. It is science itself that has made death possible through these means, for prior to the industrial age, these hazards did not exist.

2) Even if you had a guarantee that you would survive to the following day, you could not be certain that there would be no impediments to carrying out the intended action, such as a sudden illness, an unexpected engagement, or some disaster. For this reason, the most judicious and resolute thing to do, is to hasten to do good and discharge your responsibilities, and the silliest and laziest thing is to delay and postpone your duties until the opportunity slips out of your hand, and you begin to complain of work overload, as the poet says:

"The day's duties, out of lethargy, I'll postpone not till tomorrow;
For, verily, the day of the lethargic is ever on the morrow."

And another poet says:

"Take care of the duties of today and expect not a tomorrow,
For who'll stand answerable for the events on the morrow?"

One day the Prophet (peace and blessings of Allah be upon him), admonished someone. He said to him: *"Exploit five (things) before five: Your Life before your Death; your Good health before your Ill health; your Spare-time before your Preoccupation; your Youth before your Old-age; Your Wealth before your Poverty."*

A scholar once said to a youth: *"Work before you become unable to work. I desire to work today but I cannot."*

Hafsah bint Sirin used to say: *"O you assembly of youths! Work, for verily real work is in the youth."*

3) Each day has its own share of work and each time has its duties. There is, therefore, no idle time. With stress already visible on his face, Caliph 'Umar bin 'Abdul 'Aziz was advised to postpone some work to the following day. He said: *"If a single day's work overpowers me, how much more if two days' work converges on me?!"*

Ibn 'Ata says in Al-Hikam:

"It is possible, with time, to discharge (all) claims, but the claims of Time cannot (all) be discharged. You see, no time arrives but that Allah has a fresh claim over you, and a definite command. How then

do you discharge the claim of some others, while you have not discharged the claim of Allah during that time?!"

4) Postponement of acts of worship, and procrastination in doing charitable deeds, leads the Self to become accustomed to ignoring them altogether. And once a habit is formed, it becomes a second nature which is difficult to uproot, so much so that a person may be rationally convinced of the imperative to worship Allah and work righteousness, yet he finds no resolve in his heart to do so. Rather, he feels lethargic and loathsome in doing so, and if ever he gets round to doing so, he finds it extremely burdensome!

Consider the result of one who hesitates in repenting from wicked behaviour and violation of rules. The Self becomes so used to committing sins and indulgence, that it is difficult to wean it from them. Everyday, the Self becomes more and more infatuated with and dependent on those moral crimes and violations. As this happens, the gravity of these crimes increases, and their clouding effect on the heart becomes the more serious until, finally, they envelope the heart in darkness and blind it to all Truths. From that point onwards, no ray of guidance reaches the heart and no glimmer of light pierces it.

It has been reported in a *hadith*[94] that: *"When a Believer sins it marks a stain or rust on his heart. If he repents and withdraws from the sin and is forgiven the stain is washed off. If he persists the stain deepens and spreads more and more until it enshrouds the heart. That is the stain which Allah mentions in His Book: 'By no means! But on their hearts is the stain of that which they do.'"* (Suratul Mutaffifin 83: 14)

To summarise, work is an important requirement of any living human being. Therefore, the person who does no work is not worthy of living, as man is required to work so long as blood flows in his veins.

A transmitted maxim which is popular with Muslims says: *"Work for (the enjoyment of) your world as if you were going to live forever; and*

---

[94] Reported by At-Tirmidhi, An-Nasa'i, Ibn Majah and Ibn Hibban.

work for your (enjoyment of the) Hereafter as if you would die tomorrow."

Blaspheming Time

A negative and evil attitude to be avoided is that of casting blame on Time, and constantly complaining over its injustice and severity. This harmful attitude encourages people to consider Time as an oppressive opponent, an enemy lying in ambush for them, or an unjust ruler who punishes the innocent and pampers the culprit - who favours one over the other without any reason save caprice.

All these are symptoms or manifestations of the doctrine of fatalism, through which individuals and societies seek to shirk responsibility for their actions by blaming others, or blaming Time, predestination, luck, circumstances, etc.

Rather than adopt this superficial and irresponsible attitude, people of piety and good sense try to carefully consider what misfortune has befallen them, or what blessing has been withdrawn from them, and analyse it according to the causes and effects inherent in the operational laws of Allah in creation. For Time is no more than a receptacle, a medium which captures and accommodates events as they come to pass by the will of Allah, in accordance with His laws and universal principles. This is the meaning of that sound *hadith* reported by Muslim from Abu Hurairah: *"Do not blaspheme Time for Allah is Time"*, that is to say, it is Allah Who lays down the natural laws for its operation.

When the Muslims suffered reverses at the Battle of Uhud, and seventy martyrs were taken from the ranks of the heroic Companions, they began to ask themselves the causes of the wounds and tribulations that befell them. The Qur'an came with the answer:

"What! When a single disaster smites you, although ye smote (your enemies) with one twice as great, do ye say: "Whence is this?" Say (to

them, O Muhammad): 'It is from yourselves: for Allah has power over all things."
(Suratu Aal 'Imran 3: 165)

The Qur'an affirms this universal principle when it says:

"That is because Allah will never change the Grace which He has bestowed on a people until they change that which is in their hearts."
(Suratul Anfal 8: 53)

For this reason, it is more appropriate that people, in their attempt to correct a deviation and reform society, should direct blame to themselves, instead of blaming Time and *"the shortcomings of their times"*, as someone once said:

"For all the time that they've been around,
Day and Night suffer not corruption;
'tis Mankind, however, that grows corrupt."

And another person said:

"We fault our Age while the fault lies with us,
Our Age knows no fault at all except us,
The Owner of Time we disparage while He's not culpable,
If Time were to speak about us, we would be ridiculed."

Some poets and writers appear to be complaining about Time, when in reality they are criticising its people and those exercising power. They are showing their rebellion against the corruption of the society and the arbitrariness of its rulers by (apparently) blaming Time:

'I asked my Age— she' s steeped in Ignorance,
Vainglorious in Evil, a total weakling—,
I said to her, "Is there a way to Greatness?"
She replied, "Two ways: Ignorance and Weakness"!'

For this reason, it has been reported that one tyrant king says: *"Time is the King. Whoever, therefore, insults Time shall be punished!"*

It is incumbent upon a Believer, when anything distasteful happens to him, to turn to himself and search for the cause, and to turn to his Lord to knock at the door of repentance and forgiveness. He should say what his two ancestors (Adam and Hawa) said when they were driven out of the Garden:

"They said: 'Our Lord! We have wronged our own souls: if Thou forgive us not and bestow not upon us Thy Mercy, we shall certainly be lost.'"

(Suratul A'araf 7: 23)

He should say what Musa (AS), the One addressed by Allah, said when he returned from the Confidential Talk with his Lord, and found that his people had gone astray in his absence and had taken for worship the body of a calf, which could not speak to them or show them the Way. They had refused to heed the advice of his brother Harun (AS), and went near to slaying him. It was at that moment that Musa (AS) turned to His Lord in humility and supplication and said:

"O my Lord! Forgive me and my brother! Admit us to Thy Mercy! For Thou art the Most Merciful of those who show mercy!"

(Suratul A'araf 7: 151)

The Believer should say what the godly men said, even as some of them were being taken as martyrs, *'...yet they never lost heart for anything that befell them in the way of Allah, nor did they weaken (in will), nor give in. All that they said was: "Our Lord, forgive us our sins and anything we may have done that transgressed our duty: establish our*

feet firmly." And Allah gave them a reward in this world, and the excellent reward of the Hereafter. For Allah loves those who do good.'
(Suratu Aal 'Imran 3:146-148) [95]

---

[95] Note that in the midst of calamity, the Prophets and pious people do not complain about Allah or His servants. Instead, they lament their own conduct and beg for Allah's mercy. This is the highest level of complaint. Below this, is complaining to Allah about His servants, and the vilest level is complaining about Allah to His servants and blaming Him for one's problems; this is the conduct of the *Shaytan.*

"The breaths of man are his steps to his death!"

(Imam Ibn al-Jawzi in *Laftatul Kabd*)

"Wasting Time in far more disastrous than Death; for Wasting Time cuts you off from (the Good Pleasure of) Allah and (the Good Life) Hereafter, whereas Death cuts you off from this life and its inhabitants."

(Imam Ibn Qayyim in al-Fawa'id)